BEATEN BLACK AND BLUE

BEING A BLACK COP
IN AN AMERICA UNDER SIEGE

BRANDON TATUM

BOMBARDIER
BOOKS

A BOMBARDIER BOOKS BOOK
An Imprint of Post Hill Press
ISBN: 978-1-64293-851-7
ISBN (eBook): 978-1-64293-852-4

Beaten Black and Blue:
Being a Black Cop in an America Under Siege
© 2021 by Brandon Tatum
All Rights Reserved

Cover Design by Tiffani Shea

Post Hill Press
New York • Nashville
posthillpress.com

Published in the United States of America

1 2 3 4 5 6 7 8 9 10

Table of Contents

Introduction

I decided to write this book after years of trying to talk myself out of it. I had fears like most. I felt it may not be received well and could possibly fail given that this would be the first book I have ever written or even read in its entirety. Trust me, I am in no way a writer. Never wanted to be either. However, over the last few years, this drive, hunger, and motivation for me to change the world and give police a voice at all costs has come bursting out of my heart.

Have you ever been asked if you had one wish, what would that wish be? I've thought a lot about that recently. If I had a magic genie come to me and decide to grant me just one wish, I would wish for people to truly, and deeply, understand the American police officer. I mean that. I am tired of seeing only the negative side to this profession. I am tired of the smear campaign against cops in nearly every city in our country. Whether it's in the news, on social media, or coming from everyday citizens, I believe there is a great misunderstanding of police officers. Beyond the sensationalized cases and the headlines—good or bad, right or wrong—there are real people who go out every day to serve their community. Those are the people you need to understand. These are the people I hope I can speak for, because they can't always share their own stories. Their stories are good stories, and they deserve to be told.

So, here I am. Writing my first book. This book will change your life. I am sure of it. You will gain insight into who I have become, by the grace of God. The most interesting part will be the insight you gain from my journey as a black man who happened to fall in love with policing in America. My experiences will surprise you. Buckle your seat belt, make sure your life insurance is active, and have everyone in your will that you truly love. LOL. JK. Let's get into this....

Chapter One:
WHERE IT STARTED

Born and Raised in Fort Worth

We all have challenges in life; none of us get to escape difficulties. Not one person. If someone tells you any different, that person is being disingenuous at best. Stay far away from them. Believe it or not, yours truly is far from the exception. I was born into a broken family. My parents did not live under the same roof. So on and so on.... It's the same story we hear all too often in the black community. But make no mistake, I'm not here to start a pity party and hope you feel sorry for me. What's the point in that? I don't think complaining about the hard times I had growing up will do much good for you or for me. The takeaway is that I made it through and, after a few missteps, took on the personal responsibility of making choices that would help me, not harm me.

Let's get back on the topic of my parents for a minute. Neither of them had a close relationship with their fathers. And even though my parents' marriage ended in divorce, my daddy was always in my life. I was blessed even before I knew it, and that has made all the difference. Let me explain what I'm talking about when I say I was blessed.

I was around eight years old at the time. I was being a typical knuckleheaded kid: not making the best choices and spending way too much time kicking it with my cousins, who were not any better at making choices. My mama and daddy didn't think much of it because they grew up doing similar things to what we were doing.

One day my older brother and several of my cousins decided to go into a vacant house in the area to smoke weed. We knew doggone well we shouldn't have been there. We had to sneak into the house through grass that hadn't been cut in months. There were needles everywhere and clear signs that crackheads had been in there doing all kinds of nefarious stuff. So, one of my cousins had the weed, and another had a few Black & Milds for us to smoke until they rolled up the weed. I will never forget my oldest cousin mentioning that he heard noises. We all told him to stop being scared like a punk. He was adamant, but no one took him seriously. Maybe two minutes later, police came storming through the front door and windows with guns drawn like they were doing a SWAT raid on some dudes on *America's Most Wanted*.

I was absolutely terrified. I never thought they would shoot us, but I wasn't going to take any chances. Keep in mind, I was the youngest at eight; one of my cousins was nine. My brother was there; he was ten. And the oldest cousin was only seventeen. It was a mess. Kinda funny, too, though. Wait, I have to tell you this part. I was going to leave it out, but I couldn't. So, check this out. My nine-year-old cousin I mentioned before was kinda heavy, which is a nice word for fat. Well, as the police came barging in, this fool decided to run and hide in a closet. The problem was, he was too fat to fit in the closet; his backside was halfway out, and the only part of him in the closet was his head and maybe his chest. I will never forget my oldest cousin yelling at him, saying, "Get yo fat a** out that closet before they shoot you." I am laughing right now as I am writing this.

Fast-forward, after the cops got us out of the house, they handcuffed all six of us and piled us into the back seat of one police car. We were five across and then another one lying across the top of us. They laughed at us and said we looked like sardines. Today, that's pretty funny. But at the time, we were all bent out of shape about it. They proceeded to take us a short distance away to a parking lot, where they let us out and took down our information. They then put us back into the patrol vehicle three by three and drove us to the juvenile detention center.

My brother and I just knew that they were going to call my cousins' parents, who were much more lenient, and we were going to forget this ever happened. Lord forbid if they were to call my daddy! Guess what they did? They called my daddy, Mr. Tatum! My daddy showed up at that substation like Hulk Hogan. He literally yelled, "Where they at? I am going to kill them!" My brother and I looked at the detention officers like, *Are y'all going to let him take us home acting like that?!*

Believe it or not, we didn't even get a whoopin'. My father did something I never expected him to do, yet it was one of the most profound moments of my life. When we were driving home—I will never forget it—I was seated in the middle row of my dad's minivan, the kind of van that had the extra room at the top, with a TV and seats that lay down like a bed. It was white, which faded into gray, with aftermarket rims on it. It was so quiet that you could hear a rat fart. My dad slightly turned to me while he was driving and asked me point-blank what I wanted for myself and how I wanted my life to turn out. He waited for the answer, even though he already knew it. Like a lot of young boys where I'm from, I had dreams of playing in the NBA. I wanted to be just like Michael Jordan. Not only would it allow me to "Be like Mike," but it would also provide me a ticket to a better life with all the money and "the finer" things I dreamed of and saw on television. Maybe a mansion, fancy cars, nice clothes. Maybe even my own plane! Because I took too long to answer, my dad went ahead and stated in a calm voice, "You will never play in the NBA if you continue down this path." He was truthful with me and said I had to decide right then about the kind of life I wanted. It was up to me to make the choices that would lead me down whatever path I chose for myself.

That thought weighed on my young eight-year-old shoulders, but I knew my dad was telling me the truth and keeping it real with me. It really was up to me. That didn't mean he wouldn't be there, and it didn't mean I wouldn't have any help, but it did mean that I had to make some tough choices…tough for anyone, but especially for a young boy. I had to think about how I spent my time and whom I hung out with, whom I picked as my friends. I couldn't pretend my actions didn't matter and that it was all going to be some great, free ride to professional sports. Choices had results.

That was when I started making better decisions. I knew that I was getting a wake-up call and that I needed to answer. My answer was a loud YES to myself. I started to put myself first and focus on school, getting educated, and learning sports. My future path wouldn't be perfect or straight, but it was heading in the right direction.

High School Hope – Paul Laurence Dunbar

By the time I started at Paul Laurence Dunbar High School in Fort Worth, Texas, things were definitely looking up for me. I was doing better in school, and my grades were good. But the real impact on my life was sports. High school sports provided this amazing positive outlet for me, where I learned discipline, teamwork, and accountability. These were the life skills I needed to succeed, and things were paying off in a big way. I had earned a football scholarship to college, and I was looking forward to a great future. Yes, I had originally dreamed of being in the NBA, but the NFL was not a bad plan B. Right? Plus, it did not help that I was a six-foot-one power forward who could not dribble with my left hand and fouled out of nearly every game I played. In other words, the NBA was too soft for me. At least, that's the excuse I like to tell myself. LOL.

Unfortunately, sports weren't the only thing influencing me. Even with all the discipline and accountability, I was still a typical teenager adopting that hood mentality. Peer pressure played a role in my decisions. There was an atmosphere in my school that celebrated violence and the "gangsta lifestyle." I was lured into it all because it was all around me, and I allowed myself to be taken in by it. I don't blame anyone; it's just the way life was at the time in Stop 6, Fort Worth. I made some bad choices my senior year that nearly destroyed my future. Let me first say, don't judge me!

Just kidding, but this story is wild. I literally tried to fight my teacher after I threw a chair at her. Before you think I am a complete monster, let me put this into context a little. Look, I was not the most punctual person at the time. It was my senior year, and football was more important to me than this class. It was so unimportant that to this day, I don't even remember what subject was being taught. Now, when you are late to class, you get locked out until after "bell work," which was an assignment given right as the bell rang to hold students accountable at the beginning of class. The "bell work" is worth a significant portion of your overall grade. So, every time I was late, I missed points. Mind you, I was a senior and needed this class to graduate and go on to play college football. At this point, I had missed all the "bell works" allowed to not fail the class. My mama ripped my behind and challenged me to be on time before I completely destroyed my future. So, I woke up this particular morning and made sure I wasn't going to be late again. Although I was running behind and cannot confirm or deny that I was going a hundred miles an hour to get to school, I made it at least five minutes early. So, this teacher, who I knew hated me, was standing in the doorway of the classroom, talking to another student. While she was speaking with him, the bell rang. I was 100 percent sure she saw me and would allow me to walk right into the classroom due to her literally standing in the doorway, preventing me from being in the class on time. This story wouldn't be good if she just let me in the class like a reasonable person. No surprise, she did not let me in. She literally slammed the door in my face. I lost it! She was intentionally trying to fail me so I could not go to college. I began calling her names I will not share in this book, because I still don't want my mama to know exactly what I said to this lady. Mama raised me better than that. Anyway, I eventually walked away from the door but was fuming. I was going to be okay until my teammate, "Big Fish," asked me what was wrong. Then I went into a rage all over again. I picked up a chair that was in the hallway, and as the teacher cracked the door to see what was going on, I threw the chair at her, barely missing her face. That's not all. I was literally trying to run up to her and fight her. Fish had to hold me back, and I am thankful to this day that he did.

Long story short, I got expelled from school. They were originally going to make me spend the rest of the school year in an alternative school, a.k.a. *school prison*. My father pled with them, and they ended up only kicking me out for six weeks. Side note: the teacher ended up getting fired because the principal was able to determine she was targeting me *and* had been sleeping with students. Shocker, right?!

Six weeks in an alternative school was horrible. I wouldn't wish that type of drama on anyone. We had to wear uniforms and use little pencils with no erasers. Had to enter the school through a metal detector. It was first-world torture for a high school All-American football player who was pretty popular. After my time was up, I went back to school and kept my butt in line until graduation.

I know that my sports ability played a big part in my life path. Being a skilled athlete opened doors that would have otherwise been unavailable to me. But I have to say, right here and right now, that if I hadn't had my dad in my corner, I would at best be in jail, if not dead. I don't want to get too far off track here, but with everything that's going on and going wrong in our society these days, I believe that fatherless homes are one of the biggest problems we face.

Can I just talk a moment about fatherless homes? Fatherlessness is one of the biggest ailments that we face in America. If anybody wants to claim to you that they care about a group of people, that they care about our society, that they care about the youth, they care about somebody's life, then what they should be talking about is the fatherlessness that we see in this country.

Now, I think, in general, based on research, about 23 percent or so of American homes are without fathers. When you break it up into demographics, the African American community is at an astronomical number; over 70 percent of the black community experiences fatherlessness. I want to point out to you very succinctly and very clearly why it is important for fathers to be at the house. And why it is important not to have children out of wedlock, especially if you're not going to be involved in your child's life. Look, you don't have to believe me. Take a look at these stats:[1]

* 63 percent of youths who commit suicide did not have a daddy in their lives.

* 90 percent of all homeless and runaway youths don't have a daddy at home.

* 85 percent of all children who exhibit behavioral disorders don't have a daddy.

1 "36 Shocking Statistics on Fatherless Homes," Life Is Beautiful, October 4, 2018, https://lifeisbeautiful.org/statistics-on-fatherless-homes/.

* 71 percent of all high school dropouts don't have their daddy in their life.

* 70 percent of juveniles in state-operated institutions don't have a daddy at home.

* 75 percent of adolescent patients in substance abuse centers don't have their daddy.

* 75 percent of rapists are motivated by displaced anger because, you guessed it, they don't have their daddy.

Now that I have shared the statistics, who in the world in their right mind would disagree that fatherlessness is the biggest plague in America when it comes to the home and the operational abilities of young children? Especially in the black community. And this is the thing that bothers me the most about Black Lives Matter (BLM) and groups of that nature. They don't focus on what's really hurting the community. I've given you stats that are consistent in general—these are not for a specific race; these are generalized stats. Now I want you to consider the effects specifically in the black community, where black families are experiencing single-parent homes at rates upwards of 70 percent and higher.

When you look at the level of homelessness in this country, the level of substance abuse by the youth, their anger issues, and the number who drop out of high school, I hate to say it, but all of those numbers are disproportionately higher in the black community. Why am I sharing this in the middle of my story? Because it is a part of my story—the story of the communities I grew up in. And, I KNOW I would have been one of those statistics if it weren't for my father, my daddy, taking an active role in my life. We need this to change, ladies and gentlemen.

Our focus needs to be on fathers in the home. There are two ways to look at this and share the message. First, look at it from the father's perspective, talking to a young man: *You got to man up. Don't be sleeping with women that you ain't marrying. And if you happen to be in a relationship, you happen to make a mistake and sleep with a woman and have a baby with a woman you're not married to—take your position!*

I'll come back to looking at this situation from the woman's perspective a little later. For now, I'll step back into my personal story. Thankfully, I managed to graduate from high school and keep my scholarship, and I was off to college.

College - Moving the Goal Post

In 2005, I started my college career in Tucson, Arizona. I had received a full scholarship to the University of Arizona. That summer, I was one of the top high school players joining the football team. Things were once again looking up for me. Just to put my athleticism in perspective, I ran a 4.3-second 40-yard dash, jumped a 44-inch vertical leap, bench-pressed 225 pounds eighteen times, and jumped an 11-foot, 7-inch broad jump. If you know nothing about the NFL Combine, this may mean nothing to you. Just know I was a freak athlete as a high school player, with numbers that would put current NFL prospects to shame.

The first couple of years in college were crazy for me. Three of my closest friends in high school died in three separate car accidents. I was riding high on my athletic abilities and doing okay in my classes, but my attitude was still horrible. I was just not able to handle coaches yelling at me and calling me out by name. I was not coachable, and I paid for it dearly. Although my life was spiraling out of control and my destiny in football became uncertain, I was headed closer to the biggest blessing of my life, unbeknownst to me: 2008! I will never forget 2008, the year I got saved! I found Jesus and became a Christian.

I want to stop right here for a moment and share more about this pivotal part of my life. When I think about who I used to be and where I've been—especially when times were tough—I realize how incredible it is that God saved me, rescued me, and changed me. I'm gonna be honest with you, before being saved, I didn't even believe in this stuff. Maybe because so many people in churches are fraudulent these days, I don't know. Whatever the reason, I didn't even believe in this stuff…until I had a real experience and a real connection with God.

It started with a dream for me, and when I had my experience, I never saw God, the Father; I only saw Jesus. Now, in my dream, I remember seeing Jesus's face, although I don't know what He looked like. But let me tell you, when I saw that face in my dream, my soul recognized that it was Jesus. I was laying in my bed, half awake and half asleep. He didn't say anything to me, but I felt this rush go through my body, almost like something went inside of me. That feeling stayed with me, and after this dream, I was really seeking God. I wanted to go to church; I wanted to just figure out if God was real or not. I kept going back to church, just trying to listen to hear more about God. I heard the gospel for the first time at Greater Emmanuel Grace Apostolic Church, and it just blew me away. I have to tell the story of how I got baptized, somewhat by accident. Let me add that I was going to a church at the time that allowed me to have what I call a full experience. At this point, I still was just sitting back in a pew and listening. I wasn't thinking about going to the front of the church to be prayed for. I wasn't like that, but I was also trying to help a friend of mine. She was crying in the pew next to me, and I guided her up to the front. And while I was there with her, they started praying for me. I didn't expect that, but then I started feeling something.

I was not the type of dude to believe in speaking in tongues or being on the floor squirming around. That was not me. That was never gonna happen to me. But these people started praying for me, and I held my hands up and just relaxed. I relaxed my mind and stopped thinking. I stopped worrying about what everybody might think of me, this big football player at the front of the church. Then, I let go for a second, and I felt something. I don't know how to explain it, but I felt like God was dealing with me. Then the pastor, who was praying for me, said, "There you go, right there. There you go. Let it go. Let it go. Let God deal with you." So, I let go of all the distractions, and I focused on what God was trying to do with me right then. I relaxed my body, and the people there guided me to the ground, and I completely let go. I zoned out. At that point, it wasn't about the church, the religion, or anything else except God and my relationship with Him. The pastor who was there said I had to be baptized in the Name of Jesus. He commanded me, and I got up and was baptized, right there on the spot.

I want to say here that I don't pretend to know anyone else's story. I can only tell you mine, so I understand other people may have different experiences. But at that moment, when I was baptized, my mind was as open as a child's. I literally felt light, like the burdens of sin had just been washed off of me. I was also open to receiving the Holy Spirit. I knew if God was real, he was going to do something miraculous in my life. I was open and ready. And two days later, my life changed even more. The people at this church prayed for me, laid hands on me, and I even spoke in tongues—which, I have to say, is just about the craziest thing to ever happen to me. Now, I will never be the same. That doesn't mean I am perfect. I may mess up, and I have at times been in situations where the old Brandon came out. I've been riled up and gone into beast mode. But I get back on track. I mean this when I say I will never be the same. There is nothing anybody can say to me to prove that God isn't real. Nothing. Nothing. You can't tell me that I didn't experience what the apostles were talking about in the Bible in the Book of Acts. You can't tell me that it didn't happen to me 2,000 years later. This stuff is real.

Knowing I was saved, baptized in Jesus's name, and filled with the Holy Spirit had a profound impact on my life. One of the changes in my perspective is that I shifted away from the Afro-centric focus I had held my entire life. Growing up the way I did and where I did, everything was seen through the lens of being black. With that came a perceived animosity that separated me from every non-black person in my world. That's not unusual for most young blacks growing up in America today. If you get fed a diet of animosity and anger for long enough, that becomes all you see. But after being saved, I understood that we are ALL children of God, no matter the color of our skin or the depth of our sin. That may not seem like a big deal to some of you, but for me, it was a major change.

Being Christian became my first identifying quality, and I worked hard to live my life accordingly. I was able to let go of a lot of anger I realized I didn't need to have. I even became a Christian leader on the football team. Numerous players on the team began to follow Christ because of what God did in my life. I managed to get through my senior year of college without too many problems. I figured all I had to do was wait for the NFL draft to scoop me up and send me on my way, although I never started a single game. I was that confident, and so was my agent. I did have a tremendous uphill battle with a lack of film and the fact that I left the football team after the third game my senior year. That's a story I'll have to tell in another book, or you can just ask me when you see me in person. That was in 2010, and I thought I was ready for what life had in store for me next.

A Dream Deferred – A Reality Realized

I am sure I'm not the only one who makes plans only to have things turn out differently than imagined. The NFL was my plan A, but I didn't take a second of my life to consider a plan B, which was a problem considering the NFL could never be a plan A. Why is that? I'll just say it straight up: because I did not get drafted—not one team picked me up. My dream was over just like that!

I was stunned. That was a devastating blow because I needed that draft to make a future for myself—and my family. You see, I was about to become a father. My fiancée and I didn't plan to get pregnant, but that was our reality. That's one reason I know what it's like when life happens while you're making other plans. Now let me clarify that I fully faced what was happening, and I had every intention of supporting my family. However, I had just learned I could no longer rely on an NFL career to support us. I *knew* I needed to be able to provide for my family in some other significant way.

At that time, I had a mentor in my life who was a successful millionaire. He was the one who helped pick me up off the ground when the NFL draft dream disappeared. He was the one who guided me and supported me as I searched for something different to do with my life. At the time, I admit I probably wasn't searching for a career, just a good-paying job. But he's the one who helped me focus and take the steps toward what would become my career. By the way, in case you can't tell, I'm a huge advocate for mentors. I think it's vital to surround yourself with successful people. Not only is it true that you're the sum of the five people you spend the most time with, but when you're in the company of successful people, successful habits rub off on you. We learn by what we see and experience as much, if not more, than what we read or study.

Since I sidestepped a bit already, I want to get on my soapbox again and share with you why I knew then and why I still believe now that having a father is vital for a child's success. Yes, I'm coming back around to that thought.

First, my father had intervened for me in a big way twice in my life—at eight and eighteen. Second, in case you didn't catch it, I was about to have a child out of wedlock. My son's mother and I were not yet married when he was on the way. But I knew it was up to me to take care of him as we planned our lives together. I love my son dearly. Even though his momma and I did not work out, I am consistently in my son's life. No matter how much stress, no matter how much drama, I'm gonna make sure I'm in my son's life. Because when I look at those stats I shared earlier, I know there's a big chance that things will be hard for my son if I was not there. Let me recap some of those numbers: 90 percent of runaways, 75 percent of kids with substance abuse problems, and 71 percent of high school dropouts do NOT have a father in their life. So yes, I believe that being in my son's life is invaluable. No matter how I feel or how I'm getting along (or not getting along) with his mother, I need to be in that boy's life. I need to be consistent. He needs to see an example of a real man. He needs to have access to his father.

I think that all men should think that way. It doesn't matter what the circumstances are; do your best. Now I know there are women out there who are crazier than two left shoes, and they're going to make it their mission in life to keep you from your child. All you can do is do your best. That's all I'm asking you to do—at least do your best. Now, if the woman has moved out of the country and has done all this crazy stuff that women sometimes do, then at the end of the day, you should still be able to look in the mirror and say I did the best I could. I'm cool with that. I'm cool with that, brother. Some things are out of your control, but you should be making a concerted effort to be in your child's life because of those stats I shared. Each one is somebody's child.

Remember when I said there are two ways to look at this scenario, the first being from the perspective of the father? Well, the second perspective is from the woman's side and about becoming a mother. I'm just going to be honest right now. Women, I am about to get on some of y'all—stop sleeping with men who ain't about nothing. Don't sleep with a man who's not married to you. I am sure you've heard the saying about why would a man buy the cow if he's getting the milk for free. I am *not* labeling any women out there, but please think about this. If you don't demand to be respected, and if you don't expect him to behave responsibly, how can you be surprised when he owns no responsibility? So please quit putting yourself in positions where you're allowing yourself to get pregnant by a low-life, losing, sorry son-of-a-gun who was nothing when you slept with him—he ain't gonna be nothing when he moves to New Mexico or wherever!

Now, I know there are situations out there that are a whole lot more complicated. Maybe you were in love, you got married, and things fell apart. Maybe you don't want to risk being hurt again. But just like I said to the men, women, do your best. Make it your priority to be sure that your child has exposure and access to his or her father. Bottom line, at the end of the day, when you look in the mirror, you should be able to tell yourself, "I did all that I was supposed to do." It's not about your feelings or whether or not you like the joker. None of that matters. Let me clarify something because some of y'all are going to say, "What if he's a criminal?" If the fool is a criminal, he's not a father. If the joker is in and out of prison, he's not a father; he's a sperm donor. I'm not talking about those fools. I'm talking about men who are actively a part of their child's life—who want to be a part of their child's life. They are fathers. Just do your best to be intentional. It's invaluable to have a father for young girls and young boys.

You may be thinking, "Why do you say that, Brandon?" You may wonder why I've stepped up on this particular soapbox in a book about being a black cop in today's America. I do this because it's an important part of the story. Because for young men, it is irreplaceable. Let me say it again for the people in the back. It is irreplaceable. You cannot supplement the feeling that a young man has when he visibly sees his father. I mean just on the visual, just to see your father, just to see an example of who you can be— it's invaluable. To see a man who looks like you and with whom you share a bloodline and a family name—even without words, that means everything. And then to have a father who shows you compassion—I think one thing people forget is that the love and intimacy that a father shows his son are invaluable. Because when young men grow up without that love and that compassion from another man, they begin to look for it in other areas. Sometimes that's abusing women, sometimes that's being promiscuous with women, and in many cases, it's being promiscuous with men. They're trying to look for that God-given connection with that source. And without it, they end up going astray.... Remember the stats I shared?

What I'm saying is there are certain things from a man, from a father, that you cannot replicate. And, while I'm not here to speak for everyone, I speak not only from my own story but also from the story of so many young men I interacted with throughout my career as a police officer. I read those sobering statistics, and that data says fatherlessness is the number one thing that creates destruction for young people in this country. And I know for a fact that every young man—and it was all young men—I arrested were juveniles who never knew their dad. They had never met the man and didn't know who he was. So, for me, it's more than just numbers on a piece of paper. I've experienced it myself, and I met many of those "statistics" and looked into their eyes and felt their pain. Being black in America and how you end up relating to authority—and, in my case, the police—it starts with fathers.

Whew! That's a lot of soapbox preaching. So, let's get back to how I recreated my future. How did I go from a down-and-out football player who lost the dream before it happened to a proud police officer? It might have been sheer panic! I was a young man about to have a young child—a baby—depend on me for *everything*! Of course, he would need his mother, too, but I had to provide the financial stability and security it takes to raise a family. Knowing football was over in a flash, I had to move on. I didn't have time to feel sorry for myself, but that's not to say I didn't have a pity party or two.... I'm only human.

My amazing mentor helped me look at all my options, because my vision had been pretty narrowly focused on sports before. He helped me take one step at a time to find a new direction and focus. So, what did I do? I applied for every job I could think of that would provide not only wages but benefits. I applied everywhere, including the police department and a few other places. I felt like a job with the city would fit the bill if I could get hired.

One evening, while I was just waiting and hoping for a response to *any* of my job applications, I got into a huge argument with my fiancée. I was so frustrated and wondered, once again, what was happening to me. I think there was a part of me that still felt life happened to me, and I didn't have much say in how it was going to happen. Then I realized that was all wrong.

The next morning, I got a call from the Tucson Police Department. At first—I'm not going to lie—I thought that call was because my fiancée called the police on me. I was like, *This chick called the police on me over an argument on the phone.* However, I got offered a chance to complete the application process. Let me tell you that as an eight-year-old arrested for smoking marijuana, a high school graduate who almost lost a scholarship, and even a college football player hoping for the NFL draft, being a police officer—a cop—was not on my radar. Luckily, I was smart enough to recognize that opportunity when it came to me. Needless to say, I said YES in a big way, and it became another turning point that changed my life.

Chapter Two:
BECOMING OFFICER TATUM

My First Hero

Before I get into this chapter, I want to debunk a myth that has been bothering me for years. I am almost certain that you all have heard this crap before. People are out here saying that the profession of policing came primarily from slave patrols. Let's put this old dirty lie to rest right now. First of all, the first police force of sorts was actually composed of volunteers who worked part-time to look after colonists, making sure they were not engaging in gambling and prostitution. In the early 1600s, Boston started incorporating "night-watchers," and shortly after, around 1650, New York followed. This method ended up not being effective because many of these night-watchers would get drunk and do nefarious things due to a lack of adequate supervision. In some cases, being a night-watcher was associated with punishment and not a desirable part-time gig at all, which had nothing to do with slaves. However, there were slave patrols, which were only in the South, where their primary economic interest was to preserve slavery. The first sign of slave patrols in the South came nearly one hundred years after the concept of night-watchers in the northern states. During the Civil War, the military took up the primary duties of policing in the South.

Are people now willing to say the history of the military is associated with slave patrols? Of course not, because they do not have a vested interest in destroying the legacy and reputation of the US military at the moment. After the abolishment of slavery, police patrolling in the South did focus on segregation, and the police force did unfairly target free slaves. But the first formal publicly funded police department was established in the early 1800s in Boston. These officers had no involvement in slavery and were primarily responsible for protection shipments and cargo interests in the northern region by way of Boston. To sum this up a little, it wasn't until the twentieth century that we saw professionalized policing like we do today. The structure today is incredibly different from watchmen and slave patrols. The true visual representation of police evolution from slave patrols is similar to how Christians would articulate humans evolving from monkeys. It didn't happen. Although there are similarities that some would love to draw a connection to, there is not one ounce of evidence that reveals the hybrid police force they are attempting to recreate in their minds—the same way there is not one trace of the human-monkey hybrids. This is a fancy way of saying there is no notable period where slave patrols transitioned to modern policing. They are two different species. Now, I could write an entire book on this subject, but I want you to read the rest of this book. So, let's get back on topic here.

* * * *

Remember now, being a cop was never on my radar before I applied to the City of Tucson. I never knew a police officer, and my only experience with the police was when I was eight in the back of a police car in handcuffs and a few minor traffic stops. Clearly, I did not know much about policing. The little that I knew wasn't very positive, but I was eager to find out more. After I got that call, I showed up the next day at the police department. If I knew then what I know now, I wouldn't have done what I am about to describe next. I just drove right up alongside this random police car. Let me repeat. People, please do not just approach a police car if that officer has no idea who you are or why you're coming toward them. That can be an aggressive act, something that never crossed my mind back then.

I was lucky, and everything turned out fine. That's because the cop sitting in that car, Officer Sean Payne, was an amazing man and a great cop. In fact, he was my first hero; that's how awesome he was. Our initial exchange went something like this:

"Wassup, can I do a ride-along?" I asked.

"Can you do what?" replied Officer Payne.

"Can I do a ride-along with you?"

"Are you interested in being a police officer?"

"Yes, I already filled out my application."

"I see. Well, meet me here tomorrow, and you can do a ride-along with me."

I did just that and met up with Officer Payne for my first ride-along. Now, the day was to be nothing special; it was just going to be an average day in the life of a Tucson police officer, I thought. It started out slow. We stopped to help an elderly woman change her tire. I didn't know cops did things like that, but I thought it was pretty cool. Helping other people, even with the little troubles in life, seemed like a good thing to me.

Then things changed. There was a call over the radio about a young man in trouble. We sped off down the road Code 3—lights and sirens blazing. We were on our way to save a young man attempting to commit suicide! The call came out stating that the young man was actively cutting his wrist.

When we arrived at the location of the incident, Sean and I got out of the patrol car and met up with several other police officers. They all took off toward the young man's apartment. I trailed behind them, looking as goofy as you-know-what. As they approached the front door, they had me stand at the end of the stairwell about thirty feet away. I saw them force entry by kicking in the front door after their knocks went unanswered. Once they entered the residence, I was able to run up and peer through the doorway. I saw the young man with a knife in his hand, cutting at his wrist area. I couldn't believe what I was seeing. Sean Payne was able to secure the knife from the young man and save his life—literally. Ladies and gentlemen, for the first time, I saw an actual hero.

I will never forget thinking to myself, *This dude does this every day.* Not once a career. Not once a year, not once a month, but every day! Even though I was slightly terrified, by the end of the day, I knew this was the kind of life I wanted to lead. I wanted to be a hero! I wanted to help people in my community with all God had put in me to give. To be able to be the person someone turns to in a time of need...that sounded better than the best day of being a pro football player. Not that I have anything against athletes—but football is a game. Policing is real life where wins and losses are attached to life and death. There's a big difference.

Without question, I finished my application and showed up at the testing facility with great joy and honor in my heart. Let me add that the process is grueling. It wasn't just an easy waltz through the park. However, I subsequently went through the academy after making it past the application process that took months. Let me tell you, that experience could have its own chapter. But let's finish this. I worked hard, finished strong, and became an official Tucson police officer in 2011, class of 11-02! After basic training, I didn't stop excelling. I took advantage of every opportunity to learn a new skill and improve my rank within the department.

My Track Record

One of my proudest accomplishments was joining the SWAT Team. It was the most challenging yet rewarding training I've ever experienced. It was probably similar to the "Hell Week" (not quite) the Navy SEALs experience. But instead of cramming it into one week, we got our butts kicked over three weeks. I also became a field training officer, which involved training new officers in the field to be heroes like myself and Sean Payne. After only two years, I also spent a year as the department's public information officer, speaking on behalf of the Tucson Police Department. So much for white privilege and black oppression (which I think are made-up terms meant to divide us)!

I enjoyed all the training I got in the department. I don't think anyone would disagree with me that no matter your opinion of cops, we all want active officers to have excellent training. That's what I provided. I really enjoyed being an officer, and I wanted to do what I could to ensure the department always had well-trained rookies joining the force. Instead of complaining, I took the time to teach the things I'd learned, to make us all better and more equipped to be excellent to the citizens of Tucson.

Another important part of being a police officer for me was my connection and relationship to the community. I was blessed to be popular and well-liked in the department, but I was perhaps even more blessed to have a strong relationship with the community I served. I got to be that positive example of cops out in the street. And, I'll admit it: I like positive attention. That's why I was tapped to be a spokesperson for the department. Whenever a message needed to be delivered to the public, the department asked me to do it. I spoke to the press. I spoke to the public. I ran our social media, and I made videos. Overseeing social media and making videos would eventually become a big part of what I would do, and I'll share all those details with you.

My Most Memorable Moments

Man, when I think back on policing, I think of all the fun times that we had in the squad, like when we would prank each other and joke in the briefing room. It was such an amazing time in my life. I have to say that one of the most memorable experiences for me was just putting on that uniform every day, putting on my Axe body spray—so I would smell good when I'm on patrol, you know—and getting suited up and ready to answer the call for service. I would get in my car, put my music on, and take a deep breath. Then I'd grab myself a drink from the QT and head out to conquer the city and answer the call. That daily routine was my favorite part of being a police officer. Thinking about how many people I could reach and serve each day. How proficient I could become, how much I could improve as an officer, even how I could write better case reports—every detail was wonderful. But just like any police officer, there are some specific cases and special moments that always come to mind when I think back on my career.

The first case I recall is one I was very proud to be a part of as an officer. It was pretty well known at the time: the Sophia Richter case. This is the case where the parents had held their children captive for years. The girls couldn't see each other, couldn't go outside, and they were malnourished. It turns out the parents had done this in multiple jurisdictions. But it just so happened that on one of my night shifts, Officer Cuestes and I were on patrol, and there was a call about a domestic violence situation. A young girl had jumped out of her window, run to the neighbor's house, and said her dad was chasing her with a knife.

We showed up at the scene, and it was more than a typical domestic violence call. In fact, she had escaped captivity. She had been locked in a room, and somehow, she was able to get a window open. Her stepdad heard her trying to leave but couldn't stop her. I think he tried to kick through the bottom of the door to get to her in the room. Luckily, she was able to get out of the window and run. She managed to save her youngest sister as well. They both jumped out and took off to the neighbors. They had to leave their nineteen-year-old sister in the house because she was in a different room. But we got there, and after talking to her, we arrived at her house—I think right when the dad was cracking up and about to lose it.

We ended up arresting him, no question. The condition of those girls and the rooms they were kept in were horrible. I will never forget how badly I wanted to choke this man unconscious for what he and his wife had done to those three girls. The older girl who had been left when the younger two escaped was unrecognizable when we rescued her. I mean, she was no more than seventy pounds. She was nothing but bones. They had starved those kids, locked them in rooms, wouldn't let them see each other, and supervised their bathroom visits. It was horrible.

You know, when we arrested him, he spit on my uniform, like we were the bad guys. He was a horrible person. But we were able to save those kids. And we were able to get those children justice against that monster and his wife. And when I testified in court on that case, it felt really good to see those two go down. Plus, we were able to arrange for those girls to see one of their favorite rock bands and have some VIP treatment. That was a little bonus to provide them some fun and happy memories.

That was one of those life-changing cases. But I also remember my first high-speed chase, which happened during my field training. I mean, I'll never forget that. We were headed in for a briefing, and the day was over. Normally, we dedicate the thirty minutes before a shift and the final thirty minutes of the shift for briefing. It's a time to calm down and go over special details about the upcoming shift. And it gives you an opportunity to decompress and transition between you and another shift because they have thirty minutes to transition in, and you have thirty minutes to transition out. So we were transitioning out and had about ten minutes, maybe just five minutes, to go before we were set to leave. And we heard a call on the radio that said a man had stolen a pickup truck, at knifepoint. He was heading westbound on Prince Road.

I remember thinking, *That's toward our substation. There is no way this guy is going to go right by our substation. No way he's going to go down and turn right toward us, is he?* Immediately, the air support unit was activated, and there were already five units behind that guy. My FTO—Field Training Officer—said, "Don't worry about it. We're going home. They've got this. Just chill. We're going home." Then, all of a sudden, we heard that the guy was changing directions and getting closer to us. Now he was about three miles from the substation. He was continuing westbound and approaching Flowing Wells, which is where our substation was located.

Just like that, two officers on my squad jumped up and headed to their car. They said they were going to get back into it. My FTO looked at me and said, "No, we're staying right here. This is not going to go far." We kept hearing updates about the roads he was on and the turns he was making. It was crazy. Then they said he was getting ready to pass Code 12, which was our substation. And I will never forget this. My FTO looked at me and said, "Let's go! Let's go." So, we jumped in the car, with him behind the wheel. I'm still mad I didn't get to drive. We got to the gates, and as soon as they opened, we saw the suspect fly by the front of our gate. He just flew by, and there were about five or six units behind him. We're not supposed to do that, but they were doing it anyway. It's supposed to be only two units in a chase, but you know, when the chase is on, everybody's jumping in. We ended up jumping into the high-speed chase too. As soon as the gates opened up and the guy passed by, the commander came over the radio and said, "Pursuit authorized. Pit maneuver authorized. Spikes authorized." So, he authorized everything as we left the gate, and we were number nine in line in the pursuit.

And this guy decided to take the frontage road and not the freeway. Now, our department policy was that units have to come to a complete stop at every red light. Picture this, he took the frontage road, all of the other eight cars chased him down this road, but he was blowing through red lights at 80 miles per hour. All the other officers behind him had to stop at every red light, a complete stop at every red light. So, he is outpacing them by like a mile. We decided to jump up onto the freeway and ran the freeway parallel to him, going 140 miles per hour.

We caught up to him, and we passed him once, and we exited. At this point, we decided to try the spike strips. I get out of the car, you know, I'm just lighting up like a Christmas Tree. I'm a rookie. It's my first high-speed chase. It's my first time trying the spikes. But by the time I got them out, before I even had a chance to put them down, he was already passing us. So, we jumped back in the car and kept pursuing him. Now, remember, everybody else on the frontage road was still stopping at every red light, and they're stuck at a light and can't get on the freeway due to construction. Right now, we were the only ones in pursuit. Everybody else was probably a mile behind. He got off on the exit and tried to go into a residential street and ended up heading directly head on toward another car. He lost control. He hit the curb and almost flipped the truck over. We were able to use the pit maneuver on him. I jumped out of the car as another cop came up and he intentionally rammed the front of that patrol car. But we kind of had him pinned in at that point. And rookie me, I was able to get to the door first. I was able to pull him out and "gently guide him to the ground using the least amount of force necessary to execute and arrest." I don't know how but he lost a lot of skin on his forearms, lol. I will always remember that feeling. I was the bad boy, the rock star. The other cops were saying, "Rookie, handcuff him. Handcuff him." So, I was handcuffing him, and the helicopter light was flashing down on me. I looked up at the helicopter light like I was on a Hollywood movie set. It was an epic arrest, and there were a lot of cops who were a bit jealous. One guy said he'd been on the force for twenty years and had never been in a pursuit like that. He'd never been able to catch a person in a high-speed pursuit. That was a high-impact, adrenaline-filled, memorable moment.

But that's just one type of moment. A completely different moment was when I saved this lady's life. She tried to commit suicide. She lured us to her residence, which I later found out, with the plan to commit suicide by cop. She lived in a duplex kind of setup. We arrived on the scene and had a lot of what we call less-lethal munitions, meaning things like paintballs, Flex-batons, and pepper spray. We obviously had guns and shotguns, but we led and planned to use the less-lethal options so that if she ran at us, we would be able to shoot her without killing her.

I was the one that was to make contact with her, to knock on the door and make sure she was there. The other officers were to cover me. And I decided to walk up and look around at the side of the building, which was about ten feet from her front door. This was to make sure she wasn't on the side of the building while we're focusing on her front door. So, as soon as I looked around the side, I came back toward the door, and she popped out with a knife and came at me. She didn't run. She stepped forward grimacing and shaking. I could see the fear in her eyes. I could see that she didn't really want to do this. She was just holding the knife, anticipating shooting to start.

I remember pleading with her to drop the knife. I kept saying, "I don't want to hurt you." The odd thing is that in this instance, I thought back to my training, but it was real now. This was not a fake person at the police academy. This was not someone who worked for the department and was role-playing for training purposes. This was the real thing. She was a real person having a real life crisis. As that realization hit me, I had to step up my game and understand that this was life and death, and her life was in my hands. If I could negotiate with her, she would live. If

I couldn't, I might have to kill her. And you know, having to look into someone's face and coming to the conclusion that I would have to kill this person—that's very difficult. So, I'm looking at her; I'm giving commands; I'm using my crisis intervention training. I'm talking to her, and I'm pleading with her. I think it took about ten minutes of this, and then she just threw the knife down.

It was one of the greatest moments of my life, you know. She was going to try to get us to shoot her. I was thrilled we didn't. My training worked. All of the other officers were shocked. And we were ready to take her into custody. I personally took her to the mental health facility.

Another great moment for me was when I saved this kid from jumping over a bridge to her death. Many times, when people are suicidal and committed to ending their lives, they don't call 911, they just do it. But when they're looking for help, they call and say, "I want to kill myself." They are really reaching out for somebody to help them. The people that don't call are the ones who have already decided to kill themselves. This situation was one of those. This young lady, who was sixteen or so, was right by our substation on Miracle Mile. She was up on an overpass that goes over train tracks. It's probably a thirty-foot-plus drop to the train tracks below; it could have even been higher.

The call came in that a young lady was hanging over the edge of this overpass, that her feet were dangling off the edge. It looked like she was gonna jump off the bridge and kill herself. Now, she didn't call the police. Instead, it was the people passing by that called it in. I just so happened to be right by the substation. I was the only officer in the area. Everyone else is about two or three minutes away. The other officers that were on the way didn't want to put the lights and sirens on. They didn't want to spook her because she might jump off. So, I pulled up, probably about forty yards away from her. I pulled off the roadway where she couldn't really see me. She was focused, looking at her legs that were hanging out.

I remember walking up to her and thinking, I only have one chance at this. Either she was gonna get spooked and jump to her death, and I'm gonna live with that forever and have to go down and try to assess her mangled body. Or I'm going to save her life. Or we're both gonna fall. And I thought, *Well, I can't fall with her.* I am just going to creep up on her. I decided that when I got close enough, I was just going to go for it. I wasn't going to say anything to her. I wasn't going to talk. I was just going to go for it. I was going to lunge at her and sweep her with my forearm over and around her while I fell toward the ground, away from the edge. If she slipped out of my hands, I know I would have tried. If I caught her, I'd be a hero.

I remember saying to myself over and over, "It's gonna work. It's gonna work." I ran up to her, and I got my forearm out and just sort of swept her off the bridge. I ended up rescuing her. I remember picking her up and hugging and holding her like she was my own kid and saying, "It's gonna be okay. You're gonna be okay." She was crying. I also helped transport her to the mental health facility. Those two moments—when I saved someone's life—are two of my happiest moments.

* * * *

Making a difference in someone's life is one of the best things about being a police officer. But sometimes, you don't know if you're making a difference. There are a couple of times when I found out later how someone's life changed because of what I did as an officer. One time, I was at a gas station, catching up on business paperwork and getting ready to go inside to get something to drink. My guard was down, you know. I'm looking down at my computer, and suddenly, this kid pops up in my window. I almost put my gun on him because I don't know what to think. Was somebody about to rob me or ambush me? I looked up and grabbed my gun, ready for whatever came next.

Then this kid's face was in my window, and he said, "Mr. Tatum! Thank you so much, man. You changed my life. You arrested me the other day for having marijuana. I quit, man. I quit after you arrested me, man. I quit. I don't smoke marijuana no more."

I was caught so off guard, but when he said those words, I teared up. I told him how happy I was for him. Just seeing how I impacted that young man's life was amazing. At the time, I had been feeling bad for arresting him for marijuana. He was this young kid, and I thought, *Man, I hope he turned his life around.* And then for him to be so excited to remember me and run up to me at a gas station…. That was amazing.

I had a similar interaction with another gentleman. He was a military veteran who had PTSD, was schizoaffective, and had a lot of other mental health issues. He was off his medication, and he began to panic. He thought he was at war. He was low crawling in his backyard with his rifle. He thought he was right back in a combat zone. Of course, the neighbors were freaking out and called the police. Because of the situation, SWAT was sent. At that time, I was responding as a member of the SWAT unit. And I think he fired one shot at some point before SWAT got there. We were able to rescue him, but we had to confiscate all his guns. And I remembered seeing his work truck in his driveway and thought, *There goes his job.* I felt so bad for this guy who had served our country. Now he was in such a state of distress. I knew he wasn't really harmful. He was not going to hurt anybody. He was just mentally messed up. After we saved him, he went to a facility without incident, but I was really sad for him.

A while later, I was at a gas station, and I saw that work truck pull in. We both went into the store at the same time, and he looked at me like he knew me. "Officer Tatum, I remember you." Wow. I remembered him instantly. He said, "Oh man, you guys changed my life, man. You saved me, man. I got my job back. I've got all my guns, you know, I'm on my medication, man. Thank

God y'all didn't shoot me, man." When I got back into my car, I was tearing up again. Here was this man who just needed help, you know. And now he's got his job back, and his life is back on track. I thought he was done for, and he'd be institutionalized, but he got his life back, and that was great to see.

I have so many other stories, but those are just the ones that tend to come to the surface. When I first became a police officer, I was so inspired. I was so excited. I felt I was called to do the job. When I was a rookie, I didn't want a day off. When Friday came, I couldn't wait for Monday. I would take my police radio home and listen to it all weekend. I could not wait to get back to work.

When Monday came, I was excited. I mean, I was there, I was ready to go. I couldn't wait to ride in my own patrol car, just feeling the breeze, being in nature, interacting with people of all backgrounds. Being able to help, being able to be a hero, being a light in the darkness and a time of weakness for a lot of people…. It was just such a beautiful experience. I remember everything about it, like kissing my son goodbye as I was ready to go to work. It truly was one of the best times of my life. I met so many great police officers. I marvel at the great people I was able to work with, the amazing men and women who put on the uniform. They're just regular people, but they stepped up to do such meaningful work. They were all heroes to me.

I think it's obvious, but I'll say it right here one more time: I loved being a police officer. After six and a half years and doing nearly every job I could within the department, I didn't have any specific plans to leave the force. However, God led me in a different direction. It was all connected to making videos and sharing my thoughts. I didn't just speak for the police department. I also had started my own personal social media page and started posting my thoughts and perspective. Today I have a lot of followers on my social media platforms—even though it wasn't always that way—and these days, I have been asked about a thousand times, "Brandon, why did you leave the police department?" "Why are you no longer a cop?" "Did you get fired?" "Did you do something wrong?" "Was it too dangerous?" "Could you not be a conservative in the police department?" All those questions have been posed to me, and I want to share with you the answers to all of them before I go any further with this book. Ready? Here we go!

Once a Cop, Always a Cop

No, I did not get fired. And no, it wasn't because I couldn't be a conservative in the police department. Actually, in the Tucson Police Department where I worked, they loved me. Everybody loved me; everybody loved "B. Tatum," as I was called. Remember, I was the voice of the police department. If they wanted something said about the chief, about white privilege, about the tax on law enforcement, B. Tatum was making a video! Commanders all the way up to right under the Tucson police chief really liked and appreciated me. I will admit right here that I didn't get along with the chief too well. We had different views on just about everything, but even that is not why I left the department.

Now, back to my explanation. It wasn't any of those negative things. It really had nothing to do with that. The full story is that before I was making a lot of videos, I was mostly sharing my thoughts and opinions through written posts. Now, I've always been outspoken, but up until 2016, most of the things I spoke about on my Facebook page were about God and my faith. I would normally just post and write something on Facebook about what I was feeling or something I wanted to say. At that time, depending on the post, maybe a hundred people would like it, which was a lot of people for me. While I love that I have so many more followers now, back then, that was a whole lot of people. If a hundred people liked a post, I thought, that's great.

The other thing that started to happen was I was becoming more conservative in my political views. Some of that started when I heard then-President Barack Obama say negative things about the police. I really believe that having what I felt were "anti-cop" things coming from the President of the United States began to create an environment where our job was way more dangerous than it should have been. There were always those who disliked the police, and I know there always will be, but that lack of support from the highest office in the country did some damage. I refused to support that.

Then my police buddies were like, "Bro—you're not a Democrat, I don't know why you think you're a Democrat. You're a Christian. You're pro-law enforcement. You are pro-life. You're all these other things. You're not a Democrat." Mind you, I was taught that I was a Democrat my entire life. My entire family claimed to be Democrats. I was taught by my peers that Democrats were for the people, especially black people, and that Republicans were racist white people. But through the seeds planted in me by my coworkers (mostly Officer "Woody" Parker), I finally opened my eyes to the truth. So, as a police officer and truly seeing what mattered to me, it was a bit like the scales fell off my eyes. That was when I said to myself, *Let me go to this Trump rally this week and see what he's all about.* I did not start out supporting Donald Trump; I was a Ben Carson guy at first. Then when Ben Carson dropped out, he supported Trump. So that's where I was, truly a bit undecided, when I opted to go to this rally and see if Trump was even serious. He was speaking at this event in Tucson, so it was easy for me to attend. I was absolutely shocked at what I saw. Trump ended up not being who they said he was. He was not a racist, and his followers were everyday Americans like me.

Now, the protesters were absolute lunatics. They were threatening kids and elderly people, blocking the entrance, and just being evil. After that event, I said to myself, *I need to post about what happened at this Trump rally.* Writing a post wasn't good enough. I had to make a video. This was actually the first video I posted on my page. I thought it was only going to be seen by approximately one hundred people who always saw and commented on my stuff. I was *wrong!* The video went viral, so much so that I thought I was going to get fired because millions of people were watching that video. It was such a big deal that I was asked to be on a few news shows on Fox, including *Hannity* and *The O'Reilly Factor.* O'Reilly was still on Fox when this happened. The other show that wanted to book me and talk about this viral video was *Fox & Friends.* Many news outlets were already sharing my video, but these shows wanted to actually interview me. I was amazed and more than a bit taken aback. But I was excited by my unexpected fame.

Then the bombings in Brussels happened. News is an ever-changing medium, and the terrorist attack in Brussels was a bigger story than mine. So, they had to cancel nearly all my appearances. Still, one show wanted to keep my interview—that was *Fox & Friends.* The crazy thing was this was to be a live interview, which meant early morning news on the East Coast. That meant a super early morning for me. I wasn't worried about being awake; I worked the graveyard shift. I was worried because I was at work. I was on the job, ladies and gentlemen! I did not want to miss out on this cool opportunity, so I asked my boss if I could take some time off. I wanted to take off for two hours and then come back. He agreed, so I took leave for two hours. It was about two in the morning for me (Arizona time). I ran into the locker room, took my uniform off, dressed up in my suit, and then hurried to the studio. At the studio, I recorded my bit, went back to the station, changed back into my uniform, and went back on patrol. The rest of that shift was odd because some people recognized me. I was getting looks, double takes, and a few "Hey, you were just on TV, bro," or "What the heck? Didn't I just see you on TV?"

That's how it all started. I became one of those internet sensations but with a unique viewpoint. Initially, I had decided I was going to stay a police officer. I had no desire to be anything else. I told myself and others, "I'm going to be a police officer." I had gone to school to get my master's degree so I could be a police chief. That was me. But I kept making videos, and I kept being the life and voice of the police department.

Things were moving along just fine, and then one day, Colin Kaepernick happened. I should thank him because, in my humble opinion, the only good thing that came from him taking a knee is that it changed my life. You know what I'm saying? Of course, I made a video. Of course, I ripped his behind so badly in that video. Of course, that video went viral. That one video had about seventy million views on Facebook. Both from my own page to other pages and sites that grabbed and shared my clip, I calculated about 70 million views. It could have been a lot more. That, my friends, is a lot more than a hundred!

When that happened, it was like hitting the big time. Suddenly, everyone knew my name, and I had organizations and groups that wanted me to be their spokesperson. That was when I left the police department. It was because I had an opportunity to do something different and new. I agreed to be the spokesperson for a company called Conservative Tribune. This is a sub-online news station that is affiliated with Liftable Media and The Western Journal. Many of you have probably heard of at least one of these media outfits.

However, even when I left to work with Conservative Tribune, I didn't really think that I would do it long-term. I thought I would try it out and see what happened. I want to be honest with y'all—one of the deciding factors was they were offering me a financial package that I couldn't refuse! I was going to make almost $20,000 more per year than I did as a police officer. And my signing bonus with them was almost more than I made in a year as a police officer. I couldn't refuse that. Remember, I had a family to support. So, I thought I'd try it for a year and just take a break. I was still a certified police officer, and if I didn't like the whole spokesperson thing, I was 100 percent okay with going back to patrol.

But God began to open up even more things for me. I ended up working with Turning Point USA. You've probably heard of the founder Charlie Kirk and Candace Owens—those were the amazing people I was working with. I was speaking around the country, something I could only have dreamed would happen. My social media was growing, and things were just moving on-ward and upward. I believe God was showing me that He wanted me to expand and to go in a different direction. I was now able to do more things and be more vocal. I had a chance to change the world, not just one sector of the Tucson area between nine at night and seven in the morning. You know?

I am so grateful for what God has done in my life and the opportunities I have to reach out to people, meet them in person, and talk to them. As I've tapped into being a true entrepreneur, there are a lot of business ventures happening. I started to imag-ine I could even have my own private jet—one of the dreams I had when I thought professional sports was my future. But these days, I want to make money for things way beyond some new toy I could buy. I'm about to launch a nonprofit organization (in the end, we win), an energy drink (Tatum energy) and I hope to be successful enough to just give money away to people—money that can change and impact people's lives for the better. I want to be a blessing to others financially, and that's something I couldn't do on a cop's salary.

However, once a cop, always a cop. I am still connected on a deep level to the police officers who put their lives on the line every single day. I understand their stories and what they go through. I want to be a part of sharing those stories and helping them make the difference they dream of as well. When someone decides to be a cop, it's to serve others. It's about protecting their community, keeping people safe, and being that hero for someone—like my first hero, Officer Sean Payne.

I don't think enough people really understand what it's like from their side of the uniform. That lack of understanding is part of why too many wonderful police officers are feeling beaten down, disheartened, and defeated. I want to lift them up, share their experiences, and help the rest of America get to know these amazing officers. I believe there is hope for the future, for better relationships between officers and citizens. I hope the following stories do just that.

Chapter Three:
POLICE BRUTALITY

Let me start by saying this right out loud: Yes, there is police brutality in America. Yes, there are cases of misuse of force and use of excessive force. I'm not going to lie and try to say it's not true. But please read this: policing in America isn't systemically racist and they are not riding around looking for black men to kill. Not every shooting by a cop is a bad shooting. There are justified shootings and unjustified shootings. The most important thing to understand is that every case is unique, and as with any situation that has two sides, you've got to be sure you hear and understand both sides. Makes sense, right? I do not understand why every person in America doesn't understand this. I want to jump right into this and go over some of the cases getting the most media coverage. I will talk more about the media's role in all of this in a different chapter. Right now, I want to share some details so you can better understand the reality of these situations. Better information helps you make better decisions.

Two Sides of the Coin – George Floyd and Derek Chauvin

Yes, I'm going to start with the biggest case in recent history. May 25, 2020 is the date that a lot of things changed for America. It changed for police, it changed for black people, and it changed for non-black people. There's a lot to unpack here, so let's get right into this. I call it the tale of two idiots. This had nothing to do with racism on the part of Derek Chauvin. The other three officers did nothing wrong. Now that I got that out of the way.

For six and a half years as an officer, I had no formal complaints against me. Why? Because it's really not that hard to treat people with respect. It's really not that hard to not break the law or to not do something that's against policy. It's really not that hard. And even if an officer has a few complaints, I get it. No one is perfect, and sometimes a good cop makes a mistake or messes up along the way. They're probably still a really good cop. But Derek Chauvin had so many complaints that you have to take a beat. I can hardly believe I'm saying this, but he had eighteen complaints over a twenty-year career. Sixteen of those were dismissed without action, so I can't speak to the details of those complaints. But understand that a police officer having that many complaints is unique—and not in a good way. When you look at the number of complaints he had, plus his behavior with George Floyd while people were recording him? I don't even know what he was thinking! Was he smoking crack? I mean, what world is he living in? In what world is it okay to have your knee on someone's neck like he did? Then you add the fact that he was surrounded by tons of people yelling and recording him, pleading with him that George was dying and for Chauvin to at least render aid. Even if there was a training policy like that, he knew what it looked like. Didn't he have to know what it looked like?

Even if he had to kneel on George because he was acting out, what this officer did was wrong on more than one level. His knee should have been lower, closer to his upper back. George Floyd was in handcuffs. He was lying face down with his stomach down on the ground. There were two other officers on his legs. People were recording him, and Chauvin knew that. The crowd was responding to what they thought they saw in his behavior. It was over the top. It was excessive force. I just have to wonder how things might be different if he had just chilled out a little. I don't mean just for George Floyd and Derek Chauvin. I don't even mean just for the other officers. I'm talking about our entire country. This incident was a powder keg that resulted in riots and violence exploding across our country for the rest of the summer and beyond. Would those riots have happened anyway? Maybe, I can't be sure. But maybe not.

But they did happen, and those initial riots were kicked off by one man, one police officer, who was extremely arrogant. Was he just trying to show what he could do? How far could he go? Was he trying to prove something? In my opinion, he showed he was a dummy. He was fired, and all of the other officers were fired for the part they played in this mess. However, the other officers were not in the wrong in my opinion.

He's facing murder charges for being stupid. I mean, if only he had just paid a bit more attention to all the cameras and all the people yelling at him to stop. Right? He could have eased up on his neck because it was clear that, at a certain point, he and the other officers had the upper hand and the leverage. George Floyd wasn't going anywhere. It makes me mad to see Chauvin's behavior because it makes all cops look bad and heartless and stupid.... When I was a police officer, I was in situations that were way more violent than that, and I would never do to anybody what Chauvin did to Floyd. I just wouldn't.

I also think George Floyd was an idiot. I know everyone wants to make George Floyd a martyr to the cause of police violence and brutality. But he wasn't innocent. I'm not saying he wasn't trying to get his life on track, because I don't know him personally. But on that day, he was backsliding for sure. He was not just a black man walking down the street, minding his business, when here come the racist bad boy cops. That didn't happen. That hardly ever will happen in the history of our country. It won't happen most of the time. George Floyd was trying to purchase items from a store with fake money. He tried to take advantage of a local business and pass fake money. So, he was the reason the police showed up. He set this thing in motion. The cops were probably minding their business at the donut shop. Yeah. And he had to waste their time trying to buy something with fake money because he was high on meth and fentanyl. He made a stupid choice and got called out on it. When the cops showed up, he started immediately resisting. It started at his car. The officer, who wasn't Chauvin, had to put him at gunpoint because he was being uncooperative and not showing his hands. When the officers tried to put him in the car, he kicked and squirmed and fought back. He said he was claustrophobic and couldn't be in the back seat of the cop car. But he could be in the front seat of the little SUV he was in…crammed in with other people? That doesn't quite ring true, does it?

Listen, man, whether claustrophobic or not, one thing we know is that he had ingested drugs that were not helping him. They could have, and probably were, contributing factors to his paranoia, poor health, and his death. His choices were not good choices. Does that mean he deserved to die? No! Only God can make that judgment. However, Stevie Wonder could see that his choices had a major contribution in his death. There does need to be better training and more support for police officers. There also needs to be more accountability with the media and the role they play in creating the racial divide in America. I think they do a lot to keep Americans angry and upset with each other. But that's another book.

As I am writing this, the trial has concluded, and Officer Chauvin was found guilty on all charges. However, there's a lot of speculation as to whether Chauvin got a fair trial. Juror 52 was revealed to have misled attorneys during jury selection. He was seen in photos explicitly supporting the Black Lives Matter organization and taking a clear position in favor of George

Floyd before he was ever selected to be a juror. Juror 52 also had a podcast-type show where he spoke about the incident and gave his opinion. More controversy surrounds the fact that the venue was not changed and that the city paid the Floyd family out $27 million before jurors were even selected. Congresswoman Maxine Waters was on camera threatening more violence if jurors did not convict Chauvin. President Joe Biden and many other politicians also suggested that the outcome must be a guilty verdict. The judge also did not sequester the jury, which ended up being a horrible situation in this case. Lastly, there were alternate jurors that made statements of feeling intimidated and like they only had one choice, and that was a guilty verdict. Chauvin's lawyers filed for an appeal referencing a mistrial, which is still pending as I'm writing this.

Facing Reality - Breonna Taylor

The next case that received a lot of news coverage is the case of Breonna Taylor. Why? Because what I'm still hearing and seeing is not the truth. They're still lying about this case. Ladies and gentlemen, I'm gonna just say this right here, right now: Please don't believe the lie that Breonna Taylor was just an innocent young black lady sleeping quietly in her bedroom. That she was asleep and dreaming about her idyllic future because she had turned her life around. And that the police suddenly and accidentally kicked her door open and bombarded her apartment. That is not what happened.

I have reviewed forty-plus pages of documents related to the investigation into Breonna Taylor, JaMarcus Glover, and other conspirators involved in an active drug ring. Breonna Taylor's residence, her person, and her property were on a legally obtained search warrant to raid her house. The police were not at the wrong address, as some have said. She was involved—knee-deep, ankle-deep, crochet-braid deep—in the drug game with JaMarcus

Glover. She got caught up in that, and unfortunately, she lost her life in the midst of it.

Now, her boyfriend, Kenneth Walker? I think he should have been charged for his part, but I can understand how, with the totality of circumstances and the "beyond a reasonable doubt" threshold, he wasn't charged. I get it. Everyone else heard them knocking, and even though some of the neighbors said they didn't hear the police announce themselves, that doesn't mean they didn't? What we do know is that when the door opened, Walker looked at Sergeant Mattingly, and he shot him. We also know that in Kenneth Walker's original statement, he said that Breonna was the one that did the shooting. He blamed her for it, said it was her fault, and said she was the guilty person. That is until Sergeant Mattingly spoke up and said he saw Walker point the gun down the hallway directly at him and shot him. Mattingly basically said, "He shot me. I saw him shoot me. I returned fire." Unfortunately, it seems that Walker was shielding himself behind his girlfriend, Breonna Taylor. She took the rounds right on the chin, and probably one to the head. That's not the police's fault. The situation, sadly, is the cost of doing business when you're involved in a drug gang. It's a tragic result of a series of bad choices.

But there's something else I've got to say. I do not believe that Breonna's life and choices would be so examined and criticized to this particular degree if it had not been for the Left trying so hard to defend her. I think if Breonna Taylor was viewed like every other person that this happened to—and yes, situations like this have and do happen—it would have been chalked up to a situation gone bad. Instead, people were pumping up and promoting her as a complete innocent. Some folks act like she was a god that had done no wrong. That's where the problem of the truth comes into play. As the facts were exposed, the way the media and the Left painted it was all wrong. Let me hit you with some facts.

Fact: She wasn't sleeping in the bed; she was up and in the hallway.

Fact: The police didn't hit the wrong house. They had a legitimate search warrant for her residence with her name on it.

Fact: The search warrant did have a no-knock exception, but the officers went ahead and knocked anyway. Then they blasted through the door because it was necessary.

People, listen to me. The Left and the media were, and some still are, lying to the masses about who Breonna Taylor was and what she represented. It's shameful, and I think you need to know the truth. That's why I posted all the documents on my website, TheTatumReport.com. I mean the whole gamut. I don't want you to just take my word for it, and I really don't want you to only rely on the mainstream media. I want you to have access to the truth. Please, do your due diligence. Read the details, and share them with your friends, your mama, your baby daddy, everybody you can, because people need to know the truth.

It's unfortunate when stuff like this happens. And it happens all too often. People shield and protect people like Breonna Taylor. When they do that, they lead people astray. They lead black people astray. They lead us down a path of destruction because they never address the real problems. They only address the police. And when the police aren't the problem, then what do you have?

You end up with what I think was a foolish decision, a brain-dead decision, where people talk about abolishing the no-knock warrant. I want to share some more facts right now. But before I do, please ask yourself some questions. Ask yourself: Have you ever conducted a no-knock warrant? Have you ever been a part of a no-knock raid? Have you ever been a part of an investigation that necessitated a no-knock warrant? If the answer is no, then just take a seat, chill out and keep reading. Understand that a no-knock is probably one of the proficient ways to do a warrant when you're dealing with violent people. Think about it. You don't want to knock on somebody's door when they know they're about to spend the rest of their life in prison. They have enough time, motive, energy, and effort to do you in while you're knocking on the door like a peaceful person. And I want people to understand that a no-knock warrant is used in a lot of different situations. It's not just used for drug-related arrests. It's used for the people who are watching illegal things online, things that involve little kids. Imagine what would happen in a situation like that if the police just knocked politely on the door?

Knock-knock. It's the police. The person on the other side of the door hears: *You're about to do the rest of your life in jail.*

Knock-knock. Mister? It's the police. Open up. The person now hears, *Not only are you about to do the rest of your life in jail, but we can't be sure that nobody is going to take advantage of you while you're in prison.*

Oh, and go ahead and wipe the computer before we get in there. Go ahead and do whatever you got to do to hide evidence.

Are you beginning to understand? That's what can happen. No-knock warrants are for cases where you know you have some-body doing felonious things or has felonious material on their computer. In other words, they have evidence they can destroy, delete, or flush down the toilet. Instead, the speed of surprise and action police use with these warrants completely overwhelm people. They have no way of knowing what is happening to them. They think you're coming in the front door; you go in the back door. They think you're coming in the back; you go through the window. If needed, you throw flashbangs. You do it all, so they don't know what's happening. They don't know if they're asleep.

They don't know if they're alive. They don't know if they're in hell. It's the element of surprise. They've got a whole bunch of things going through their mind. By the time they figure out what's happening, the police already have them on the ground and arrested. It's that fast.

And before police execute a no-knock warrant, they do a lot of evaluation. They don't hit a house if there are kids present or if there's even a possibility of kids being present. You know, they check the address 1,000 times. They do what they call drive-bys. They drive by and check it out. Make sure it's all good. The suspects never know it's the cops, but that is what's happening. The police have to take all kinds of steps and precautions before they serve a no-knock warrant. They do that to be sure, to be as sure as they can be, so they come out on top and not get served a bad hand.

I'll wrap this up by saying again, please be sure you have all the facts before you decide who's guilty and who's innocent. Please don't assume the police are always in the wrong and always the problem. Reality proves that's not true.

The Edge of the Knife – Justified Uses of Force

Now it's time to shake things up a bit more. Like I said before, there are cases of police brutality, and there are times when even good cops can step over the line and use excessive force. I promise you; I'll share some of those stories with you. There are also times when police officers are justified in their use of force and the actions they take. I already talked about Breonna Taylor's case and explained that the police did nothing wrong in that situation. There are a few other instances I want to review as well. I'm gonna talk a bit about Jacob Blake, Elijah McClain, and Philando Castile. Please understand that I am not doing this to upset anyone or push any emotional buttons. My goal here is to help people understand the complexity of being a police officer. You cannot make policing all good or all bad. It's about the facts, not feelings. Let's get into this.

JACOB BLAKE

I'll start with another case that got a lot of media attention: Jacob Blake. After the way the media portrayed him, people wanted to worship him as a living black god. The easy thing was to look at him and make your judgment based solely on his skin color. Forget his actions. Man, MLK must be spinning in his grave right now. People, without checking the facts, swore up and down that he was innocent. He didn't do anything wrong. He was just trying to see his kids. People, please!

Did you know that he wasn't even supposed to be at that house or in that city? He had a zone restriction that he violated by being at his baby mama's house. He wasn't even supposed to be in Kenosha, but there he was. His baby mama is the one who called the cops on him, because he wasn't supposed to be there, and she didn't want to deal with him. So, the police show up to arrest him, and it doesn't go well. He was not trying to break up a fight between two other guests. I don't even know how that lie started. Blake immediately begins to resist the arrest. A fight starts, and he's fighting back against the cops. They try to tase him, but it doesn't work. Nothing works. And this just blows my mind: people swear he didn't do anything wrong. They swear before the living God that he was just walking to his car. Whoever said that should be ashamed. Some athletes had his name on their helmets. Those folks should be ashamed of themselves. If you were a pastor at a church and you said Jacob Blake was some type of martyr, that he was an illustration of police brutality in America, I think maybe you should renounce your credentials, lay them on the ground, and forfeit your church to a real pastor.

That may seem extreme. But people, we have got to wake up and look at the facts. Everyone said he was so innocent and that he did not have a weapon when he resisted police officers.

Are you kidding me? He admitted it himself on national television in an interview with Michael Strahan. And his reason is probably the dumbest excuse I've ever heard. He said he dropped his knife while he was fighting with the cops. Did you get that? He admitted he had a knife while he was fighting with the police. He realized he dropped it when he got up off of a police officer after he'd been tased. Oh yes, he was tased because he kept fighting with the police who were there to arrest him, and he had a weapon in his hands.

It gets better, or should I say, worse. Remember that his three boys were in the car, and so far, all this fighting and scuffle took place on the passenger side of that car. You would think, at least I think, a caring father would want to protect his kids first and foremost. But not Jacob Blake. He says in this interview that he picked up his knife and decided the smart thing to do was ignore the cops telling him to drop the weapon and walk around to the driver's side of the car. He opens the driver's car door and claims he was going to just lay the knife down in the car and then give up and allow himself to get arrested. None of this makes sense. Why pick up the knife at all? Why not just let yourself get arrested?

Let me recap this for you. A few months earlier, he had committed assault against his baby mama. That's why he had a zoning restriction against him, meaning, he couldn't even be in Kenosha. He showed up, and his baby mama called the cops to arrest him. They showed up to do just that, but he fought back, even putting one officer in a chokehold. He kept fighting, and the cops tased him twice, but it didn't stop him. He dropped his knife during this, picked it up, and walked around the driver's side of the car. He ignored orders to drop the knife, risked getting shot, risked the lives of his three kids in the car so he could put the knife on the floorboard. That's what he says he was doing.

But I just have to ask, what was he thinking? I mean, why was he fighting so hard? Why was he so desperate to get that knife and get to the driver's side of the car? Was he gonna try to pull off with the kids? Was he going to hurt those kids or put them further in danger? What did he think was going to happen? Yes, the police shot him as he leaned into the car. He had proven he was gonna keep resisting, and they had a job to do. Enough said.

ELIJAH MCCLAIN

Now I want to talk about Elijah McClain, a young man who lost his life in 2019 while in police custody. If you are not familiar with this case, Elijah McClain was walking down the street after purchasing something from a store. He had on a ski mask and hoodie, I understand because he was anemic and got cold easily. There was a 911 call made because some people in the neighborhood thought he looked suspicious because of the ski mask and his actions or behavior. Obviously, the police officers are going to take that call seriously. They wanted to figure out what was going on, so they found him and stopped him on the side of the road. You can look at the police bodycam footage of this, and you'll see the officers approach him. They were very calm. They were kind. They were reasonable. They asked him to stop a few times before McClain complied. He immediately began arguing with the police, who repeatedly said they needed to detain him because he'd been acting suspiciously. He didn't want the officers to touch him because, he said, he was an introvert and wanted space. He resisted the officers while they tried to detain him and, unfortunately, but not surprisingly, there was a physical altercation.

During the altercation, he kept tensing up and resisting. The officers got McClain to the ground and supposedly used what they call a carotid choke, which caused him to pass out temporarily. The officers commented on McClain's super strength, which made them wonder if he was on something. When the EMTs arrived, they gave him a therapeutic dose of ketamine, a sedative to calm him down, so they could safely transport him. Once in the ambulance, he ended up having a heart attack on the way to the hospital. He was alive when he arrived but passed away six days later. There's a lot of emotion around this case, and too many people love to find yet another case of violence against black men. Truth time! This had nothing to do with police misconduct. The police were doing their job. He resisted arrest; they held him down and the EMTs gave him ketamine. The toxicology confirmed it was a therapeutic dose and not enough to kill him. No matter what people might feel, it was rightly decided that there were no charges against these officers.

It is an unfortunate situation. I'm sad. It's sad that this kid lost his life. But in cases like this, there is a common denominator here that we see more often than not. It's that people are resisting arrest. I don't understand why people continue to do this. Stop resisting arrest, people. When an officer says stop…stop! Even if you believe you're in the right and that they shouldn't be arresting you, stop. And then, please, have your day in court for wrongful arrest. But if you resist arrest, if you get into an altercation, you could die. I would much rather see people fight against a wrongful arrest than fight the cops and end up dead. Believe me, nobody wants that, especially the police.

We do not need people mislabeling every altercation and every arrest as another case of police brutality on a black man. If you're doing this, you should be ashamed of yourself. You are the reason that our country is so divided. Look at the facts and do your research before you make a stupid argument that should not be made. Are there things in the police department that can be improved? Of course. But you know how you don't end up in an altercation with the police? You don't resist arrest, whether they are detaining you lawfully or not. That's something that you determine in court. If you keep fighting, then you're gonna keep getting the same results.

PHILANDO CASTILE

I wanted to touch on the details surrounding Philando Castile as well. I wanted to make sure I succinctly described and defended my position because I know there are people out there who think differently on this one. But I want to focus on the facts here. Let me say right now that I agree his death was tragic. Still, based on the police's explanation and the facts, which I'm about to share with you, I agree with the prosecution that it was a justified use of force. Unfortunately, it resulted in the death of Philando Castile.

Let's start at the top of this thing. People are saying that he had no priors. Okay, you need to understand that doesn't mean you have not committed any felonious crimes, it just means they haven't caught up with you. It doesn't mean you aren't doing any crimes. I mean, he's openly smoking marijuana with his baby in the car, which is a felony crime. And, in Minnesota, smoking marijuana in general and being in possession of marijuana are felony crimes. So, there is evidence right there that he was committing felony crimes. Another thing that you probably don't know is that he'd been pulled over forty-nine times. As a former cop, that fact makes me wonder about him. I don't know what he was doing to get pulled over forty-nine times, but my instinct and experience tell me something is wrong. It can't always be someone else's fault that a person gets pulled over that often.

It was also said he had a legal concealed carry weapon permit, or a CCW. Well, let's take a closer look at that. It was argued in court that he wasn't legitimately in possession of the CCW because he was using illegal drugs, and illegal drugs were in his system when he obtained his CCW permit. Most folks don't know this, but on the application for a CCW, you have to disclose whether or not you're currently using illegal drugs. If you're currently using illegal drugs, you can't get a concealed carry permit. He was a drug user, so he lied on his application. That's a crime.

Even if he hadn't lied, having a CCW comes with responsibilities. When you are carrying a firearm, it's your responsibility to carry it in a holster. You don't carry a firearm in your pocket. Is it against the law to carry a firearm in your pocket? No, it's not. But is it smart to carry a firearm in your pocket? No, not in any way. It can easily fall out, something or even someone brushing up against you could cause the gun to go off accidentally. A person with a CCW has some responsibility. If you carry a gun, secure it in a holster, and, if you need to use it, you can pull it out very quickly and safely.

Okay, back to the traffic stop. According to court documents and the officer's testimony, Philando Castile was reaching for what most people believe is identification or something that's in a console. Simultaneously, his gun falls out of his pocket, and from the police officer's viewpoint, it appears that Castile is reaching for the gun. Castile did not respond to the officer's commands. Now, his response could have been too slow because Philando Castile was high, I don't know. Still, he continued to move toward the gun as the officer was yelling commands. I believe that the officer did think his life was in danger at that moment. Now, I don't believe I would have shot him in this scenario, but I wasn't there. I have a lot more tactical experience and am confident using my firearms and the tactics I was trained to use. However, I was not there, and I was not in that officer's head. I believe he feared for his life.

Philando Castile lost his life, and the officer lost his career. People may judge the officer, but that's neither here nor there in a court of law. The police officer was acquitted, and I believe rightly so. It's a sad tragedy at the end of the day. What you had was a person making so many poor decisions that he was pulled over forty-nine times. He lied on his application for a CCW permit and was in violation of a CCW permit by possessing marijuana. He was high when he was pulled over, had weed in his car, and he was carrying a gun. Altogether, that's a crime he knowingly committed and would have been arrested for that day. Nobody wants to talk about that because it's easier and causes more division to make him an innocent victim of police brutality. But let me be clear that Philando Castile was no martyr. He was not a victim.

Overstepping – Unjustified Use of Violence

I told you I was gonna keep it real, keep it 100. I will always focus on the facts and tell people the truth. There are some people—I know, because I've heard from them—who think I blindly support all officers and rally on the side of cops in every single case. That's just not true. I say what I say and stand where I stand because I know exactly what I'm talking about, and I understand the facts. Some people call me an expert, but I just say I know what I know, and I know what I've been trained to do. I did this for a living, and I know police policies and procedures. That's why I shared with you the facts about Derek Chauvin and George Floyd. It's why I can speak the truth objectively and share with you some other cases where the police made bad calls and mistakes. Again, I want to talk about these situations, so people won't blindly jump to conclusions and assume they know what's what…when sometimes they don't know anything at all. Once again, let's get into this.

LAQUAN MCDONALD

I know what I'm talking about in the Laquan McDonald situation that occurred in Chicago. After I read the case, I immediately said this officer was going to be charged with second-degree murder. Now, with every situation, there are multiple things to consider, and I'll break it all down for you. The officer, in this case, was wrong. I'm not standing up for somebody if they're wrong. This case is about the level of use of force.

I'm not going to paint a pretty picture for civilians or police in this case. I'm just going to paint the truth. This cop, former officer Jason Van Dyke, was charged with second-degree murder.

First, let's look at the criticism he received from his radio transmission before the shooting. Look, I know officers sometimes say, "We may have to take this guy down," or "If he does XYZ, we may have to kill this guy." I get that, the adrenaline is pumping, and officers are trying to think three or four moves ahead. But because he said it over the radio and broadcast those intentions, it could be used against him in court as premeditated actions.

The other problem was what this officer said happened when he got out of his car. He was disingenuous about his interaction with Laquan. He said Laquan was attacking him. He wasn't. He was walking away from the officers when Van Dyke shot him. He was justified in shooting him, which I'll get into shortly. But he shot him sixteen times! No other officers shot at Laquan. He had no excuse for shooting a kid sixteen times. This was not a training issue. This was not a police issue. This was a personal issue.

Before I get back to the problems with Officer Van Dyke's shooting, let me dispel any fantasies about Laquan McDonald. First of all, his shooting had nothing to do with race. Laquan McDonald was high on PCP, one of the most hallucinogenic drugs created. People have superhuman strength when they're on PCP. I've seen people get shot seven and eight times and keep fighting through because they're on PCP. It makes me sad and even angry that no one wants to talk about the epidemic of black people using PCP in the black community. When someone is high on PCP, if they aren't stabbing police officers, they're stabbing their brothers and sisters. Yes, Laquan McDonald was a danger to society. He was trying to attack police officers and was a danger to the community. Laquan McDonald was not going down that night without getting shot, period. He was not going to comply. He was not going to do what he was supposed to do because he was out of his mind. He wasn't gonna listen to police officers. He wasn't gonna listen to his mama. The cops were gonna have to shoot him. He wouldn't want to just stop. He wouldn't walk himself to jail. So yes, inevitably, he would have been shot.

Now, back to Van Dyke and the use of force. Sadly, as I said, Laquan wasn't going to stop until he was shot. So, Van Dyke was justified in initially shooting. But I will say again, he shot Laquan sixteen times. Laquan went down after about the sixth shot, but Van Dyke kept shooting. Laquan didn't have a gun, and he couldn't throw his knife at anyone. The continued shooting was unacceptable. Let me give you a bit more information. People who don't understand how police training works sometimes ask me if the number of shots matters. The number of shots fired, in and of itself, doesn't matter. When an officer is trained to shoot, contrary to what many believe, they are not trained to shoot to kill. That is not in any police manual or training. You shoot people to render them no longer a threat. If you shoot a man one time, and he drops the knife, you don't shoot him twice. If you shoot him five times and he dies, you don't shoot him six times. If you pull a gun on a man, and he drops the knife or drops the gun, you don't shoot him at all. However, if you're shooting him, and he doesn't drop the knife, you keep shooting him until he drops the knife. It isn't about the number of shots fired. It's about the threat. If you shoot a guy, and he's clearly not a threat anymore, and you continue to shoot him, you've gone from use of deadly force to murder.

With Van Dyke, he was charged with murder because he intentionally shot that man until he died. He shot him, and Laquan dropped to the ground and dropped the knife. He was no longer a threat. But Van Dyke kept shooting. That is called murder, ladies and gentlemen. People have a problem with the police because they are not informed. They don't understand policy and procedure. Each situation where violence is used is unique and complicated.

I want to share two more thoughts about this case. First, the majority of police officers are people of integrity, people of training, and people of sound mind. Officers know how to shoot someone five times instead of sixteen and are good at perceiving threats.

These officers, 99 percent of the time, are doing it right. They're not found guilty because they're not guilty. Secondly, if you cannot see that Laquan McDonald was a problem because PCP is destroying our communities, you may be a part of the problem. If you don't see anything wrong with a person brandishing a knife and running around terrorizing the city, you are the problem. That boy was addicted to PCP, and it ruined his life. What are you doing to help him or to help the next Laquan McDonald? Please, don't just sit around and blame the police officer. You need to be blaming the fool that's selling these young people PCP.

WALTER SCOTT

Another case I want to touch on is the 2015 case of Walter Scott from Charleston, South Carolina. This man was initially pulled over for a broken taillight—there's nothing too odd about this because that's something the police can see when they're patrolling the streets. At first, things seemed to be going smoothly. But once again, panic and bad decisions changed the outcome. Now, I'll say right here that Walter Scott wasn't perfect. He was behind in child support payments. I've said earlier how important I believe being a good father is, so I don't condone him not paying for his babies. But I also don't know his circumstances and why he owed back payments, and I don't know how behind he was. So, why do I bring this up? Because his fear of being arrested for owing this money probably played a role in his actions.

Okay, so Officer Michael Slager pulled him over in the parking lot of an auto parts store and approached the vehicle. He got his ID and walked back to the squad car to run Scott's driver's license. This is when Scott seemed to panic. He jumped out of his car and started running. Officer Slager chased after him. It's about here that a bystander started to videotape the incident on her cell phone.

Slager pulled out his taser, fired, and then there was a physical altercation. Slager said that Scott took his taser at this time, and the officer feared for his life. When Walter Scott ran off, the officer fired at him. He fired eight times, and five of those shots hit Scott, who went down. The cop approached Scott, radioed that the subject was down, and that Scott had taken his taser. He walked over to Walter Scott, who was face down on the ground at this time, and ordered him to put his hands behind his back. Slager put handcuffs on Scott, and the video also showed Slager going back to pick up an item on the ground as another officer arrived and placing it at the feet of Walter Scott. It was later discovered that the item was the officer's taser.

It's no surprise that Slager went to jail for killing Walter Scott. And this was the right call. I am not sure if Scott really tried to take the taser, but there was a struggle over it. Officer Slager may have thought he actually had it. By watching the video, it looks to me like they fought over it, and it dropped to the ground. That's the item Slager went back to pick up.

Slager pled guilty and was sentenced to twenty years. This again is a case of excessive force. Walter Scott was running away from Slager, who was not in any danger. Yes, if Walter Scott had just stayed in his car, things would have ended differently. If he was gonna be arrested for back child support, jail would have been a better outcome than death. But he didn't have to die, and Michael Slager didn't have to shoot and kill him. Bad choices, panic, and excessive force...these three things don't mix well, do they?

Chapter Four:
THE MEDIA'S ROLE IN CREATING THE DIVIDE

By now everyone knows the power of the media in crafting a narrative. They have the power to silence voices they don't like, share their feelings and perspective regardless of facts, and manipulate the public opinion of what matters and what's important. This is done even if they tell lies that they barely—and sometimes never—retract when the truth comes out. This power to make up the message also plays out on social media, where voices that don't follow the approved narrative are banned. I think it's obvious that they're doing this to keep right and left, or conservative and liberal, voices as far apart as possible. But let me tell you something else: the media is playing a huge role in the racial divide. Mainstream media no longer hides its allegiance with the Left. They've done a pretty effective job of brainwashing people to listen only to them and ignore any other perspectives as racist, wrong, xenophobic, or whatever label they can throw out there.

The media is also playing a role in the way the public views police because of the stories they cover and the way they share statistics. Most people are not going online to verify what the media says or the slant they take. Did you know that in 2019, police killed a total of 1,003 people in the US, according to *The Washington Post*'s Fatal Force database? Of those, 250 were black and 405 white. Police shot and killed fifty-five unarmed suspects, including twenty-five whites and fourteen blacks.[2] However, if you just casually watch the news or scan social media, like most people do, you might think more than 50 percent of police violence is against black people, and that nearly every time a Black person is arrested, it ends in a fatal shooting.

Why is this? Because the media is supporting the Democrats' mantra to "Defund the Police." I'll go into the ridiculousness of that in the next chapter, trust me. But I think it's important for people to have the facts. What you're getting in the media is carefully crafted to present and support a political narrative. It's not fair to the police for sure, but it's not fair to you, the American citizen. Don't you think you should be able to get objective reporting on the police? For some of you, maybe it's the first time you realized that news is entertainment, and everything on television plays the ratings game. And, because most news networks are now owned by huge corporations, it's also a financial game. These corporations donate to politicians for political power and politicians kowtow to corporations to get more political donations. It's a vicious circle that has nothing to do with the American people. Are you getting this? Are you beginning to understand what I'm talking about, or is B-Tatum tripping again? I get that some of you, or some of your friends, may not believe me, so I want to give you a few examples.

TONY TIMPA

Have you heard of Tony Timpa? If you haven't, I have a good idea why. In August of 2016, a young man from Dallas, Texas, called 911 because he was afraid and asked for help. He openly told the 911 operator that he was schizophrenic and also suffered from

---

2 "Fatal Force," *The Washington Post,* Updated August 10, 2020, https://www. washingtonpost.com/graphics/2019/national/police-shootings-2019/.

depression, but he had not taken his medicine. Now he was scared and reaching out for help. Are you with me so far?

The cops showed up to the parking lot where he was, and twenty minutes later, he was dead. He died from cardiac arrest, due in part to the drugs in his system and partially because of the stress associated with the physical restraint he suffered. Is this beginning to sound at all familiar? Let me keep going. He was handcuffed, his legs were zip-tied together, and he was put on the ground on his stomach. He was struggling to breathe, and he repeatedly said, "You're going to kill me." Oh and, the officers who were there restrained him with a knee on his back for more than thirteen minutes. Now is it ringing any bells?

If it's starting to remind you of what happened with George Floyd, you're with me. But there are some differences you need to hear about. The cops said he was aggressive and combative, but as they already knew he was an unmedicated schizophrenic, so what did they expect? Also, a private security guard had already handcuffed him before the police arrived. So, the medical responders claim he was too combative to assess, and it doesn't sound quite right. And then there's the footage that not only shows a young man in great distress but the police making fun of and laughing at him throughout the ordeal. He was given a sedative and eventually moved to the ambulance, but by then, it was too late. Tony Timpa was dead.

If you're anything like me, you might be asking why you never heard about this case. Where were the protests of police brutality? Why wasn't there any twenty-four-hour blasting of these images? Why wasn't Tony Timpa a martyr like George Floyd? The media never showed much interest because this story didn't quite fit their narrow narrative. You see, Tony Timpa was white.

Look, I'm not making any excuses for the police officers in this situation. What they did is as wrong as Derek Chauvin's actions, and in some ways, I think it's worse because they were laughing at him and mocking him. And they got away with it with a slap on the wrist. I hope there's still a chance of justice for Timpa's family. But I am perhaps even angrier that the mainstream media never picked this up and ran with it. They never had the same outrage regarding what happened, even after the footage finally came to light in 2019. What Timpa got was silence. What happened to Tony didn't fit in with the Trump-hating, Right-hating media. They were too busy lashing out at conservatives to worry about the death of another white man. Tell me if I'm wrong. Tell me if I'm tripping right now.

NORTHWEST COVER-UP

The summer of George Floyd protests and Antifa riots really brought about an ugly side of Portland, and it hasn't stopped yet. Did you know what was really going on in that West Coast city during the riots in summer 2020? Not if you were relying on the mainstream media to give you the news. The images you saw were limited; their portrayal of truth was a joke. Did you know that Portland and the Pacific Northwest is the birthplace of Antifa? They used to call themselves anarchists, but their role has always been the same: Show up at some public event and create chaos and damage. They're the group that was at the core of the Portland riots then. The Democrats who ran that city would not shut it down because they hoped it would help them win the elections and make then-President Trump look bad. Not only were the rioters and looters just practicing freedom of speech, but any efforts by the police were treated like they were jack-booted thugs and stormtroopers. The media controlled that message according to what leftist politicians wanted. Only a few brave conservative reporters were able to show you what was really going on in the Pacific Northwest.

It's not just in Portland, either, but in Seattle as well. The crowd that violently took over a section of the Capitol Hill neighborhood and called it CHOP (Capitol Hill Organized Protest) was presented by the media as another summer of love, where all were welcome. The land of unicorns and lollipops. But in the process, a local police precinct had to shut down and evacuate. This was the precinct that held the 911 call center, so anyone who needed help would just have to wait. And the summer of love resulted in violent crimes, including rape and murder. But the police were held at bay and not allowed to do their job. This was all about George Floyd and police racism, right? Then why did Seattle's first black female police chief resign during that time? Wouldn't she have been a great example of diversity? Wouldn't she have been an ideal voice to unite the two sides? Instead, she was not allowed to police the area, and during defunding budget decisions, her pay was cut below her predecessor's. The media kept pushing the message that all was well on Capitol Hill.

I believe all this Antifa action let the genie out of the bottle. After the election, on the day of the Inauguration, January 20, 2021, what did you hear about? The aftermath of the January 6th attack on the Capitol. But guess what was going on in Portland and Seattle? This group of what I have to call domestic terrorists marched through the streets of Portland shouting, "We don't want Biden! We want revenge! Burn it down!" The media seems to be totally fine with it because this is now normal. Normal? Seems to be that when you're leftist, you can do whatever you want to do. You are not an anarchistic, or domestic terrorist, no matter what you do or say. You can march and chant that you don't want Biden, the now-President of the United States. You can shout for revenge, and nobody does anything.

You might be able to find a few videos online that show you what I'm talking about. I did not make this up, the anti-Biden and anti-police messages. Oh, and by the way, they know there were evidently some BLM and far-left activists inside the Capitol on January 6th as well. One, John Sullivan, was arrested and let go for his role that day. Is that not bad enough for you? CNN and NBC paid Sullivan $35,000 for his footage, and Anderson Cooper had him appear on CNN for an interview. What? Why is someone like this given any airtime at all? But they don't bring up his role in any kind of negative way. Meanwhile, anyone on the Right that was identified was arrested and thrown in jail.

The media loves to label conservatives as fascist, but they are practicing fascism in how they practice journalism, if you can call it journalism. Think about it. If it were a group of Trump supporters walking through the street with anti-Biden messages and shouting for revenge, it would be front-page news. They would label those people as white supremacists and demand they be stopped immediately, arrested, and put on trial for domestic terrorism. But when Antifa marches, everything is fine. Nothing to see here, folks. Just keep moving along. It's like we're in Oz…. Pay no attention to the man (or media) behind the curtain.

MEDIA PUSHING ONE NARRATIVE

By the way, the media isn't just controlling the racist messaging against cops and politicians. There's a phrase: *the revolution eats its own*. Well, Hollywood and the media are no exception. Have you ever noticed that the media and the Left tend to get a little nervous around black conservatives? There are some people who actually believe that blacks can only lean to the left and vote Democrat. Really? Don't white people come from all perspectives and, politically, can be a Democrat, Republican, or Independent? Why does that seem such a strange notion for black people? It makes me mad that there's such a limiting message like that. If you don't think it's true, let me ask you something. Right before the November 2020 election, rapper Curtis Jackson (better known as 50 Cent) spoke up that he didn't support Biden because he didn't like his tax plan. As a businessman who risked losing a lot of his wealth under those proposed taxes, it's not a strange thing to say. Unless, of course, you're a black rapper. Then, your white ex-girlfriend, Chelsea Handler, has to come out and say, "I had to remind him that he was a black person, so he can't vote for Donald Trump." There's been a lot of back and forth about if he was serious or not, but I think he probably did react that way. The bottom line is that it doesn't even matter. What matters is the reality that everyone felt a black person having a fiscally conservative take on something was wrong and needed to be corrected.

Chapter Five:
BEING BLACK AND BLUE: VOICES AND STORIES OF FELLOW OFFICERS

Sharing the Real Voices of Both Black and White Officers

I have to be 100 here and assure you I know it's not all lollipops and unicorns out there. What I mean is that we all know that people are human, and humans aren't perfect. So, of course, there are people in every profession, including police departments across the country, who bring their personal baggage with them everywhere they go. Some people are going to be mean, judgmental, angry, sad, obnoxious, and, yes, racist. But as I say, overall, police are the least racist people out there because it does not benefit them on the job. Even if a few have some personal issues, rarely do you see them bring that to work.

Sadly, that doesn't stop the misguided messaging out there—the blanket statements you hear from mainstream media and the Left—that all cops are racist. The crazy thing that's been happening lately is that all these protesters, rioters, Antifa, and BLM folks shout it loudly, even directly into the faces of police officers. Into the faces of black officers! I've had some officers reach out to me and tell me their personal experiences. Before I share those with you, I have to talk about one of the craziest stories from a black officer from Portland, Oregon. His experience was blasted all over the media in July 2020, during the riots in that city.

According to the *New York Post's* reporting of the story, Officer Jakhary Jackson, a member of Portland police's rapid response team, had some unreal and what he called "frightening" encounters during the seemingly endless protests and riots the city had beginning in May 2020.[3] This officer has been on the force for nine years, and so he's used to protests, but what he said in his interview was that this time, things were different.

"A lot of times, someone of color—black, Hispanic, Asian—will come up to the fence, and directly want to talk to me: 'Hey, what do you think about George Floyd? What do you think about what happened with the police?'" Jackson said. Then, "someone white" would walk up and start saying, "Eff the police," or "Don't talk to him," Jackson recalled.

He and other officers had racial slurs thrown at them by the protesters, who were supposedly there for Black Lives Matter. I'm sorry, what the heck is that all about anyway? And Jackson went on to say that he saw more minorities among his fellow officers than he did in the crowd of "violent protesters." Jackson said, "I got to see folks that really do want change like the rest of us, that have been impacted by racism. And then I got to see those people get faded out by people who have no idea what racism is all about, that don't even know that the tactics they're using are the same tactics that were used against my people."

So, first there were more white people than black people protesting for Black Lives Matter. Second, these white people were telling people of color who were protesting that they couldn't talk to Jackson, a black police officer? And as a black officer, he was

3 Joshua Rhett Miller, "Portland Cop Reports 'Frightening' Racist Chants from White BLM Supporters," *New York Post*, July 17, 2020, https://nypost.com/2020/07/17/cop-reports-frightening-racist-chants-from-white-blm-supporters/.

both called racist and had racial slurs said to him—by the same crowd. Things are getting crazy out there, people.

I hear quite a bit from police officers across the country who share my thoughts. They say things like, "You're saying what I wish I could." Active police officers cannot always speak their mind and will not always share their personal feelings with the public. First, it can be dangerous for them, their families, and their department. Both lives and livelihoods are on the line even on the good days, but sharing certain messages increases that danger. So, I am proud to be able to speak out in a pro-police voice and share that message. And there are also a few officers who reached out to me and did want to share their personal stories. I am honored to be able to help them make that happen. There are five different stories here from five different officers. In standing with my belief that cops are one of the least racist groups of people in our country, the voices and stories are quite unique, each speaking from the heart about their experiences. Black, white, and mixed race: all are brothers in blue. Here are their stories—words and experiences that I believe will make a difference in this narrative of policing in an America under siege.

You're Black. Why Do You Want to Be a Police Officer? – The Story of Officer Lew

I guess I'll start by saying the reason I became a cop goes back to when I was a young boy, and it goes very deep. When I was about seven, I found out I was adopted. That was a shocker. I had a black mom and black father raising me, but they told me about my biological parents. Basically, my mom left me in the hospital—she left me in the hospital! I learned she was on drugs, so I was born a crack baby. Trying to process that at a young age was hard. My dad was locked up in prison, and my mom was on drugs. She just didn't want to take care of me, and that hurts. That was a problem for me, and I had a lot of resentment toward them. I was angry.

As I got older, around eight or nine, I decided I didn't want to be anything like them; I wanted to be the opposite.

Around that age, I was seeking extra attention. I would call 911 and hang up so the police would come to the house. I was in my room when they arrived and told my parents they had received a 911 call. So, of course, my parents called me downstairs and explained that you didn't call 911 unless you really needed help. But what I remember most was those officers who came to the house would sit down with me and my parents to talk to us. They took the time to care. I saw the uniform and the badge, and I instantly fell in love with what they represented. I saw them as heroes. I decided right then and there: this is what I want to do. I knew I didn't want to be locked up or anything like my bio parents. I still wanted to be the opposite of them, and in my eyes, that was a police officer. That's what drove me. I let my adoptive parents know that's what I decided, and I was determined to reach my goal.

Now I've been an officer for seventeen years and with my department for fourteen. I was a cadet at the age of eighteen and, after training, became a police officer at the age of twenty-one. Now, I'm thirty-five and am serving in the Baltimore, Maryland, area. This is where I grew up, and I'm now serving my own community.

I was pretty determined and focused on my goal, but I did get some pushback along the way. One incident that sticks in my mind was when I first became an officer. I was about twenty-one and working. I remember walking down the sidewalk in my full uniform. I had set my goal and made my goal. But this older black man walked up to me on the street. I'll never forget this. He said, "You're black. Why would you want to be a police officer?"

I was so surprised. I thought, *Where did that come from? Where does that mentality come from?* I remember thinking, *Um… so I can help people and pay my bills.* I actually don't remember what I said to him because I was shocked. I didn't know people would say that or question my choice only because I'm black.

Even today, you still get that response to certain choices you make because of skin color. Chelsea Handler, a white comedian, felt like she could tell Curtis "50 Cent" Jackson how to vote because he is black. Look at Supreme Court Justice Clarence Thomas or former Secretary of Housing and Urban Development Ben Carson. They're questioned because they have conservative values. They are looked at as "wrong" and hated by their own people. It's like you have to be a monolith and think the same and be the same. You hear a lot of people say white men pull us down. I say black men pull each other down, and that's crazy. You can't say you can blame white men for doing that when blacks are doing it to ourselves. Even rappers when they get too successful are targeted. It's like your own people say, "You can't be that successful." To me, it feels like they get jealous: you succeed, and then you have African Americans tear you down for it. It should not be like that.

* * * *

So, I want to share some insight into my experience as a black police officer. I've dealt with a lot during my time as an officer. First, let me talk about traffic stops. When I pull someone over, and they happen to be black, a lot of times I get a response like, "I was glad I was pulled over by you," because I'm a black officer—instead of a white officer. In other words, I provided some sense of relief to my fellow brothers and sisters. But I treat everyone with respect, and I think that's why I get a good response from most citizens. Yes, some of that is because I'm a black officer, and they feel I'm connected, on their side, and looking out for them. I appreciate that, but it makes me a little sad because it means there's a level of distrust for police in general. Of course, I've also heard the opposite and been told I'm a sellout because I *work for the white man.*

Let me go back to what I said about there being a distrust of police. For me, it started before the protests surrounding George Floyd. In Baltimore, and likely other places, but in my area, it started in 2014 with the Freddie Gray situation. That was out of control and was much worse, much crazier than the George Floyd situation. When those riots occurred, that's when I had a change in perspective. I just remember when the Freddie Gray incident happened. I was watching CNN, and they were live, looking at what was going on in the area. All of a sudden, people were throwing bricks at the police. I remember CNN demonizing the police. I was confused. How are they making it our fault? And I turned on my police radio and heard things I had never heard before. I heard dispatchers telling police to fall back and to stay off certain roads. I heard reports of officers being driven to hospitals. Then I heard them say officers should report back to headquarters. It was crazy. We never retreat. We move forward toward the threat. When I heard that, it was concerning. Sadly, it seemed there was no political support from the local leaders all the way up to the White House. It was a big wake-up call for me. All my life, police were the heroes, and to now hear and see this response? This world was changing.

I felt like no one in my world understood what was going on and how I was feeling. I talked to my parents, and they didn't understand. They still don't understand law enforcement, even to this day. At the time, I was dating my ex, and I don't think she was even pro-police. I was getting it from all angles—on television, in the streets, and I was not even getting support at home from her or my parents. Instead, I'd get questions like, "Why do they have to do that? Why do they have to keep shooting black people?" They'd ask these questions, not understanding at all what was really happening.

* * * *

Those riots were crazy. We would ride through neighborhoods, and people would throw bricks at the car and break our windows. We were all in fear for our lives and not able to do anything about it. Before, if someone had done something like that, I could act. During the riots, we were told to let them riot and *let off steam*. I just had to take it. I couldn't do anything, or we would be in trouble. I wondered why we were out there at all? There was anger, and many police officers wondered why we were doing this: *What are we doing it for? This is not worth it.* Based on the media and what we were told, the mayor didn't back us, and the president didn't back us. There were lots of cops asking, "Why are we putting our lives on the line when we have families to go home to? When did we become the enemy?" This is not something I started out to do. I became a police officer to become a role model. I've spoken with high school students, directly to African American youth. And they were asking hard questions. They asked, "Why do police hate us?" And I had to answer to that, you know? I was doing this and trying my best to explain what was happening because I care. I was working and taking the time to change the narrative, and it was all becoming so frustrating.

Now, fast-forward to George Floyd and 2020. It's starting to make me question again if I want to do this job anymore. This is how I felt in 2014, but it's even worse now. Now they're calling for defunding the police. We're already not funded enough, and the first thing that gets cut in "defunding" is more and better training. If you have less training, you have a worse product going out there.

I don't have all the answers, but I think a couple of things are going on these days—first, a basic knowledge that people revolt against authority. And second is accountability—no one wants to be held accountable. They want to be victims. We have a choice to be a victim or a victor, and too many people are choosing to be a victim. Everybody is struggling, and accountability is a big issue in African American culture. I'm not sure why that is; I don't know if it's solely a lack of parenting, but that's a big part of the problem—children without fathers. Fathers and stable homes make a difference. If you don't have authority in the household, you don't respect authority in the street. Police are the authority in the street, so that's part of why there's a negative issue with police.

That needs to be looked at because it's getting worse. Morale is down with any police officer you talk to these days. If they can retire, or move laterally, they do that. If they can pull back on their own effort, they do that. Now, I am not going to do that. I'm going to keep on with proactive policing. If you don't have that, it's a problem. Officers normally take preventative actions. But if you don't act when you see something suspicious, that's not good for the community. It's not good when officers feel like avoiding those things and not being proactive. That's going to affect crime in general. When cops feel good putting on their uniform, they want to go out and get the bad guys and protect the citizens. Now we don't feel the departments have our back. A cop thinks, *I could possibly lose my job for doing the right thing. Maybe I shouldn't make a lot of traffic stops. Maybe it will protect me from being sued or fired. I still have to take care of my family.* I think that's where a lot of police are today, and that's not a good thing.

It comes from misguided thought, misinformation, and what I call ignorance. So, there's a message out there that is blindly accepted that all cops are racist. I've never dealt with that or have been an eyewitness to police brutality. I'm not saying I've never heard of officers being accused of targeting high criminal areas or that they're only pulling over African Americans. Or maybe they need an arrest, so they're profiling a car because it has a black person in it. Well, I've never seen any proof of that. I don't see people talking down to citizens only because they're black. It might happen because they're a criminal, black, white, Hispanic, whatever. But in my six-and-a-half years in the department, I've never personally seen it.

As an example, I myself have pulled over a car, and the car has windows that are very dark. The driver says I pulled them over because they're black. No, I pulled you over because I can't see inside your car, and it's illegal to have your windows that dark.

Where does that mentality come from? I hate to say it, but it comes from previous generations. They are raised that way, with this counterproductive message that police will pull you over because you're black. What parents are doing is training their kids to have a victim mentality.

Parents are repeating a false message that they learned from their parents and previous generations. All it does is set up young African Americans for failure. *You have to work harder because you're black. You won't get the job because you're black. The cops don't like you because you're black.* They're training black youth to have a victim mentality. It's not productive to have us thinking like that. And then we teach it to our kids. It has to stop.

That victim mentality even happened to me. When I was sixteen or seventeen and just got my car, I was meeting some of my friends at the local gas station. It was one of our hangouts. Remember, I had just got my car, so when I pulled in, I was going way too fast. After I pulled up, before I got out, a state trooper who was there came up and knocked on my window really hard with his flashlight. He asked if I knew how fast I was driving and what the speed limit was for pulling into a gas station. I admit I was nervous. He asked for my license and registration, and then he asked me to step out of the vehicle. I thought, *Is it that serious? I have to get out of the car.* He walked me to the front of his car, and then he patted me down. He checked my license and registration and ended up just giving me a warning. I felt weird because I loved the police. But, in that moment, I did wonder if he was giving me a hard time because I was black. My friends were inside the gas station and watched the whole thing. They knew I wanted to be a cop, so their reaction was, "You want to be a cop, and this is how they treat you?" Even as a pro-police young man, I had that question in my head.

A year later, when I was a police cadet, I understood that it was just procedure. There's a system, and he did only what he was trained to do. Not because I was black, but because it was what he was trained to do. But if you put that victim mentality in there, and NOT knowing police procedure, I had the wrong idea: I think I'm looking at a racist cop then. But if you know procedure and take the victim mentality out of it, then he's just an officer doing his job! That's a memory I think about. That's what I mean when I talk about ignorance—victim mentality and not knowing police procedure.

I had a friend call me once after seeing a felony stop. He was all upset and said they pulled their guns out at him, and he didn't even have a gun. That's ignorance—that is what a felony stop is.

"That was me out there," I said.

"Well, why did you draw your guns and point them at him?" he asked.

"Well, it's called a felony stop."

"But he didn't have a weapon."

"But it's a felony stop, and that's the procedure."

When you don't know police procedure in the community, you filter things through your emotions, and you get misunderstandings. Another example is if you need to slow traffic down because something is going on up ahead on the highway (a car accident or whatever), you have to zigzag between the lines to slow down traffic. People who don't know that think the officer is drunk or impaired. They don't know you're doing what we call dragging traffic. They are leaving it up to interpretation based on emotions and lack of knowledge and mindset. So, that's why if an officer asks an African American to step out of the car, they think it's because they're black, not because it's procedure or federal case

law. I believe if we could educate citizens about some of the procedures, they'd better understand what's actually going on and make
judgments on facts instead of emotional interpretation.

Remember I said that I did get some pushback about wanting to be a police officer? Well, when you're black and young and
say you want to be a police officer, it's looked down upon. It's
like it's not cool. But along with my determination, I was lucky
enough to have a great school resource officer (SRO). When I saw
him, I thought *how cool—that's what I want to do*. He happened to
be an African American sheriff deputy, maybe only one of two in
the whole county. He was a role model for me in high school. Still,
he could have been a white cop. For me, it was just having that
positive example. It meant a lot. I can't tell you how many times I
went into his office and just talked about being an officer. He was
one of the reasons I was able to stay focused on my goal and know
it was okay to be an officer.

That's why I think it's a mistake to remove SROs from
schools. And when communities call to "defund the police," that's
one of the first programs that would be cut. Instead, we could use
those officers to teach classes or something to provide knowledge
and have some transparency in police procedure. Misinformation
and bad messaging are huge problems for the citizen–police officer
relationship. Changing that would go a long way toward making
the community better understood.

Stuck in the Middle –
The Story of Officer Ray Hamilton

My name is Ray Hamilton, and I've been in law enforcement for
about ten years. I started my career in Washington, DC, in the
Sixth District. It's where the projects are, and it's a tough neighborhood. Now I'm in Northern California in the East Bay area,
east of Oakland in the San Ramon area. I've been on the riot team,
or civil disturbance unit, in both DC and California. And for me,

a big part of my story is that I'm black and white, because that puts me right in the middle of all the race and police issues.

Coming from where I do, I tended to just assimilate the views of those around me. So, that meant I didn't really trust the police too much. When I was a teenager, I was in my car, and I got stopped. I never saw myself as looking tough or like a thug; I had curly hair and an olive skin tone. But I got stopped by the gang unit in Dallas—a true felony stop—with guns drawn and everything. "Put your hands on the steering wheel!" *Whoa*, I thought. *What in the world is happening?* "You're in a gang!" No, I wasn't, and I never was. However, my cousin was in a gang, and he used to do all kinds of criminal stuff. This was in the nineties, and things were pretty rough. He ended up getting shot five times, and he died. All that really turned me away from being in a gang or doing anything criminal.

Still, I always said I was never going to become a police officer. I did end up in the military. I was in the Air Force working for the Department of Defense on Bolling Air Force Base. At the time, I was working as a sports and recreation assistant. I created extracurricular events, like sporting events, for the Air Force community. What would come after the military I didn't really know. Then, out of nowhere, I decided to become a police officer. I believe how you do your job is more of a calling than what your job actually is. But for some reason, I got it in my heart that I was going to apply to the DC Metro Police Department. They weren't hiring at the time. And several people advised me that I didn't want to join that *dirty police department*. But I applied anyway, and I waited. I waited for two years. And most people apply to multiple departments to increase their odds of being hired. Me? I only applied to the one because I believed I was supposed to work there. And eventually, after their two-year hiring freeze was lifted, I became one of thirty-five people hired—out of about 10,000 candidates. I just believe I was led to it because I wanted to serve again after the military. And that's how I started my career with the police.

And, yes, I've dealt with different aspects of racism. I've been approached while on a routine traffic stop and admonishing somebody about some bad driving practice, and they say, "Oh, you just stopped me because I'm black." I'm like really? Because I'm mixed race, and sometimes, you can't tell what I am. On the East Coast, they thought I was Puerto Rican, and here in California, they don't know what I am. There's no box to put me in, which I think is true for a lot of people. So, when that happens, I do call people on that all the time. I respond by asking, "Could it be that I stopped you because your taillight was out, or your tags have been expired for a year, or you ran a red light? It couldn't be anything like that?" That usually turns things around, but I do have to deal with that a great deal.

When a person of color calls me—someone who is also a person of color—a racist, I feel bad for them because I feel like they're doing the same thing that they're accusing me of doing. It's like they're conditioned to believe people treat them a certain way because they are black or whatever. It's like a chip on their shoulder, and if they would stop to think about it, they'd realize it's completely unreasonable. I want to say to them, *Wait a minute. You're calling me a racist, but the very thing you're accusing me of is the very thing you don't want done to you. Like you don't want me pulling you over because you have your hair in cornrows, you're sagging, you have tattoos, you're smoking a blunt, but you don't want me to assume you're a gangster, right? You don't want me to assume that, but that's one of the first things that comes to mind. But that's not reasonable for me to do that. That's me judging you, and you don't want me doing that. So, I think why would you do me the exact same way you don't want someone to judge you?*

When it came to some of the crazy things that happened during the recent riots, one thing I think about is I am not just some overseer, which is what I've been accused of being. An overseer was someone who watched over slaves. I'm not doing that—that's not at all why I'm down there on the line. One time, someone accused me of being like the Nazis marching the Jews off to the concentration camp trains, as if I were marching people off to be killed. I was surprised by that, but it does get that dirty.

When I have on riot duty gear, or really anytime I put on my uniform but specifically when I'm on the line for riots, I remember I'm not here representing myself. I am here to try to keep some kind of peace. So, while I'm in that uniform, I don't represent my own self and my own ideas and thoughts. I'm there to protect whatever brothers and sisters are around me. We're not there to control people. I want to tell them to feel free to protest all they want. I may even agree with them, but although I agree with some of the things they're doing sometimes, I don't agree with all the methods. And I also can't let the few opportunists who are in the group cause this thing to become a mob and be unlawful.

I think it's important to hold that attitude. Because there were a couple of guys who were on the line recently and they took a knee because they were like, I agree with you, but I'm like, *No, no, brother!* You can't take a knee when you're on the line whether you agree with them or not. You can't take a knee because that puts everyone else at risk now, and we're not here to represent ourselves. It's very awkward—very awkward. It's not the time because it looks like we're not standing together. And while I was in the military for five years, and I do know how to take orders, I don't just blindly follow orders either. Still, when I'm in the uniform, I'm there for a greater purpose, and that is to keep some kind of peace and maintain some kind of order, and to do that, you have to show some kind of solidarity.

However, I also want to build a rapport with the community I serve. When I was in DC, especially in the project area, I was dealing with a different mindset. And I knew you had to meet them where they were and build that relationship. The beat I had was a very rough four blocks where there were murders, drug deals, you name it. I had a partner, and my partner was a white dude from Arizona. He'd never been around that many black people—it was an all-black neighborhood. At first, when we walked that beat, my partner kind of walked behind me. He was walking behind me, and you could visibly tell he was scared. I had to explain to him, "Dang, man, they're gonna pull your card if you walk behind me. Don't do that. If they see you're scared, they'll respond in a bad way. You gotta walk beside me, not behind me."

Since I'm in the middle—black (and white) and blue—I find myself walking the line. I know some officers have bad attitudes about the communities they serve. Yes, it's often a racial divide. Some of the white cops had a different outlook. They even made patches: *We're not stuck here with you; you're stuck here with us.* And sadly, yes, I have heard some of the guys refer to black people as savages. I'm thinking, *My gosh, how are you going to deliver or render any kind of justice or service to this community if you refer to them as savages?*

So, I'm trying to win over the white officers and the black community. Anytime something goes down, I try to give the benefit of the doubt and treat everyone the same and treat everyone as fairly as I can. Does that mean when some other officer might give someone a ticket, I would just talk to them and say what you did was foolish and give them a warning? Yes, it does, as long as what is going on warrants that. We need a lawful reason to pull someone over, so I admonish them to not give us that lawful reason. Be smart.

Sadly, I do understand why some people hate us. On one occasion, a black officer stopped a guy who was a known criminal. Everybody knew he dealt drugs, and he had drugs on him. But the officer demeaned him, I guess trying to teach him a lesson in front of the other people in the area. He made him kneel down on the concrete (that hurts), and he had him down there for more than five minutes. The crowd felt like the cop was showing off and abusing his authority. So, they started name-calling—called us "twelve," called us FEDS, called us all kinds of names. I believe when you name someone like that then they're no longer a person.

Like calling someone a savage or shouting out, "F twelve"—either side of the argument—they're no longer a person. When you can do that and make someone your enemy, they're not a person, and it's easier to hurt them.

Not too long after that, we caught a guy on a very minor misdemeanor charge, riding a dirt bike in the city. These *rough riders* would ride dirt bikes and ATVs in the city, and the cops would chase them. I caught this one guy, and we were just going to write him up, get his fingerprints, and process him out, but this guy had a $10,000 wad of bills on him. He claimed it was from his family's business. But I know that most businesses usually don't transport cash in their waistbands. I needed to hold the money until he could bring down receipts to prove it was earned through that business. He started yelling at me that he wanted to see it put in the evidence bag. I was surprised and wondered why he wanted to see that. Did he think I was going to steal it? Apparently. Because there were other cops in my district who were fired for misconduct and being dirty. So, no wonder he didn't trust us.

I can sometimes understand the lack of trust from the community, but when you don't feel you have the support of your leaders, that's when it gets really hard. When I was on the riot team in DC, we weren't able to wear our full riot gear because it looked too aggressive. And, here in California, it's more of the same. During one of the riots, I was hit with a bottle, and we had to shoot a rubber round back at that person. Then, we had to use tear gas to disperse the crowd. It wasn't three days later they took away our tear gas. I was recently deployed to Sacramento, and we were told if they break the windows at city hall to let them. We were told if you get hit with glass, we'll decide later if we'll respond with less-lethal force. Even in Oakland, we had to let them loot a Target, a 7-Eleven store, and a car dealership.

I know all the violence and looting are coordinated because I saw someone watching us and monitoring our movement. Then, he called it in to his fellow rioters. Not being able to do anything or take any action when laws are being broken and officers are being hurt? That's demotivating. You end up getting what we call 4 percent. Some officers go out on duty, but they won't be proactive, and they give less than 100 percent because it's a reaction to feeling powerless and not being supported. There's also a threat of being sued by someone, even if the officers are just defending themselves. It's very disheartening.

While I grew up feeling like I never had to be anyone but who I was, these days, I feel like I am always being forced to pick a side. I try to identify with the people I work with, and I also try to identify with the community I'm policing. I don't want them to feel like I said, that I'm just here as an overseer. I'm not here to fine you and arrest you, but I have a job to do. It can be hard to feel so stuck in the middle.

We're Human Before We're Police Officers – The Story of Officer Ryan Tillman

I am currently a police officer in Chino, California. I'm one of those officers who said he was never going to be a police officer. My dad's best friend was an officer; in fact, he was the captain of a local police department. He was always on me and kept pushing me to become a cop. I kept pushing back. I was like no, I'm not going to do that because I don't like cops. I had bad experiences with them as a kid, and I wasn't about to work for the man. I was not about to be a pig. That was my mentality.

However, I'm a huge Christian guy; I'm big into my faith, so I prayed about it. I said, "God, if this is what You want me to do, then let it be." I'll be honest and tell you the only reason I started to consider it at all was that my wife was pregnant. At that time, I was working at Abercrombie & Fitch and selling insurance. That just wasn't going to cut it financially to raise a family. So, I prayed about it, and the doors just kind of flew open for me. I still wasn't sure if it was the right thing for me, so I just continued to pray about it and be open. The doors continued to open for me, and I got hired. I ended up graduating number two overall in my class from the academy. Then I made it successfully through the field training program and became an officer. It wasn't until I became a solo police officer that I really understood my purpose within the profession, which is to bridge the gap between the community and the police.

That disconnect, that gap, is very real, and it's only going to get worse if we don't act now. One of the things that bother me is the idea that all police officers are racists. That statement is just completely false. Look, one of the things that people forget is that all cops are humans. We're humans before we're cops. We're human before we're racists. We're human before we're "dad" or "mom" or "brother." We're all human first. So, the notion that we're all racists—you can't say that because everybody is different, and we bring everything about who we are and what makes us human to the table. We all need to remember that we're human first and that we're all human—we have that in common. We need to start there, and my goal is to be an active voice in this conversation on behalf of law enforcement in the community.

These days I feel lucky to be policing in the Chino community. Overall, we have very supportive citizens. So, when the whole notion about defunding the police came up, we were able to stop it when the rubber hit the road. People realized our value, and I think it's only because we are very proactive and engage our community with everything we do as a police department. I think that's so important and has made the difference. There is a quote I like to use, which is: "You've got to get to know the community before you HAVE to know them." I think we've succeeded in doing that in our community. That's why they voted to NOT defund the police.

Still, there are some issues we face as cops and that I face myself, especially as a black police officer. I had a situation where I went to a donut shop. When I was there, a white or Hispanic guy got mad at me because I didn't have my mask on. He looked at me and said, "Where's your mask, officer?" while I was actually walking to my car to get my mask. I'm thinking, *Give me a minute, will you?* But then he added, "You're just a part of the problem! F twelve! ACAB!" And then he says, "Black Lives Matter!" And I'm like, *I know that.* I know my life matters, and here's some guy I don't know telling me Black Lives Matter, but at the same time telling me how much he hates me because of a badge I'm wearing. Those kinds of experiences are disheartening.

It's definitely frustrating to go to work. You go and show up, and you know what you're trying to do; you know you're trying to help people out, and it's just frustrating. It's kind of hard to explain. There's never a time where I don't want to go to work. I love going to work. But at times, it's hard because nobody truly understands what you're going through unless you're going through it.

I Hated Cops, Now I Am One –
The Story of Officer Mason Minner

I hated cops when I was a kid, which may make me a cliché, but it's the truth. I was one of those typical punk kids who drove a car that was too loud and too fast, and got pulled over often. I had a chip on my shoulder. It's no surprise I didn't get along that well with my dad then, and his being in law enforcement had a lot do to with it. Now I see that it was more that I just didn't understand his mindset and perspective. These days, we get along great, but as a young man, I didn't relate to him, and I never saw myself being a police officer. I was gonna join the military actually, but some things happened, and I never did that. I do remember thinking, well, now what? I ended up bouncing around all these jobs—sales, collection, and security—and as I got older, I knew I needed to figure out what I was going to do. I decided *if you can't beat 'em, join 'em*, and I figured I'd give law enforcement a shot. I applied and planned to surprise my dad, but I got turned down. I was a bit surprised, but was like, "Okay, no big deal, I'm not gonna do it."

A little time went by, and one of my dad's friends, who was involved in hiring at that time, called me and said, "Hey, do you still want a job?" At the time, I was working two jobs, both forty hours a week—so eighty hours total—and just getting by. I was definitely interested. It was not a deputy position, but a detention job because the deputy position was frozen. I was ready, so I applied. This time, I got a letter that basically said, "You're never going to get hired."

I kept doing the two-job thing for a while longer, and eventually, I got another call from my dad's friend. She said some things had changed in the hiring standards, and she really thought I could get this detention job. I decided to try one more time. I applied, went through the process, and this time, I got hired. I started a nine-week academy for that job and was ready to become a detention officer. Then, right when I was supposed to graduate, our class sergeant in charge of teaching came into the room and asked, "Who wants to be a deputy?" I raised my hand, but was thinking, *man, I do not want to get turned down again*! I found a phone and called my dad's friend. She did a quick look at my file and said it looked good for me. Within a month, I was back into training for a deputy position. With all the training for both positions, I think I basically spent the entire year training and standing at attention.

At that point, I'm about twenty-five years old, and I finally start to understand my dad. After graduation, I quickly learned how and why my dad's perspective was the way it was. I got it, which meant I got him. That made a big difference in our relationship.

I did surprise a lot of people who knew me as that *typical little punk kid*. When I told them that I joined the police force, they thought I was joking. I surprised myself when I fell in love with the job. I love the excitement, you know? I get to help people, get bad guys off the street, and the car chases, just everything. Sixteen years in law enforcement, and I still have a love for this job.

I've had a few different assignments during my time on the job, including being on protection duty for Sheriff Joe Arpaio. That's the *pink underwear* sheriff from Arizona. When I got the call for the assignment, I knew that if I didn't take on the opportunity, I wouldn't get future opportunities, so I did it. The coolest part about that job was that it was during the 2012 presidential election campaigns, so I got to meet a lot of very cool people coming through town in those days.

Now I'm on the SWAT team, but that journey was even harder than just becoming an officer. There's an annual testing for the job, and the first time, I didn't do so well on the oral interviews. Then I came back next year with a determination like I never had before, and I made the list, but they hired internally. I was a little irritated but ultimately understood. When I took another assignment, I found out it dropped me off the hire list. I skipped a year and was ready to test again, but got hurt on the job, so had to wait another year to qualify again. Seriously, it was about five years before I got hired. I'm glad I stuck with it; it's an amazing job.

So yes, I still have a love for being on the job. I love being a deputy, but these days, it is a lot harder. There's a lot of misperceptions about policing. Say that there might be one hundred people that are griping about the police and being loud, and then the media picks it up and runs with all one hundred complaints or issues. Typically, only one complaint is legitimate, right? Before, the department would take that one legitimate gripe out, give that one 100 percent of its focus, and address it. Look, I'm not denying there are some issues out there in probably every police department. But they used to be dealt with individually, separating that legitimate issue from the rest. Our supervisors all had our backs as a group, knowing most of the department was good and standing up for us. These days, it's like they have to take in every complaint, deal with them all as legitimate and give them all that focus. The response to law enforcement is we all are bad. You all need fixed, and you are all going to training. Usually training that has nothing to do with the real needs of law enforcement

It is not that I disagree with training reform. There are a lot of reform ideas that I agree with, but the big problem is that it doesn't need to come from the outside. There's too much coming from outside people that don't understand law enforcement. Remember, I hated cops, but that was because I didn't understand. When you get into law enforcement, you understand more. You get trained, and you understand why they're training you for X, Y, and Z. You know, the general public has this perception that cops have an attitude, and some guys do. When you see enough death and destruction and mayhem and violence, hear what people say to you day in and day out against you—you can become a jerk. It is hard to separate that from your attitude sometimes. That can get better, but a lot of what we're doing isn't the answer. A lot of things we're doing is not how to fix this.

I think a lot comes from the lack of quality training in law enforcement. We are so stuck on training in liability protection, and we must train a certain way to mitigate liability or negative perception, bad optics. I don't care about the optics. We need to be trained to save the lives of good people and to stop the bad guy. That's the bottom line, but it feels like someone moved the goalposts on us and made things more difficult.

Now, no matter how good a cop is, they are covered with the same misperception that they are all bad. Now, they think they're the enemy. They think nobody likes them. Yeah, there's always gonna be people that don't like us, but that umbrella of support, even internally, isn't the same. And it is changing law enforcement. For the first time in my life, I'm seeing people leave the force, not going to another agency or because they need more money. People, good cops, are leaving to go work at Costco. People are leaving to go run a farm. They're just getting out of policing. How are they gonna be replaced? When I first applied to law enforcement, there were probably 800 people applying, but just recently the Phoenix Police Department, a much larger agency than mine, only had ten. Ten!

So, what does that tell you about the culture that we've created? Before, if you screwed up, they were going to get you. But as long as you did the right thing, and you did it with a clean heart, the department would back you up. Right? It doesn't feel like that anymore. And so, people don't want that job.

They Don't Know My Heart – The Story of Officer Sean Payne

I think I'm a little bit unique in that before becoming a police officer, I had a very well-paying job. I was director of operations for a large home-building company in Tucson, but there was a part of me that always wanted to be a police officer. One day I realized, I'm getting older, and I've got to try at least. My first objective was to lose some weight. I was a high school athlete who ended up in a sedentary job. Too many client lunches, too much sitting at my desk, and I was thirty-two years old and over 300 pounds. I embarked on an endeavor to do just that, hired a personal trainer, and started working out. I did struggle some in the beginning, but I got to the point where I wouldn't miss a day, and sometimes I'd work out twice a day. I lost close to 150 pounds, and I applied to become a police officer. I was blessed and sailed through the application process. I got accepted and went to the academy. This was in 2006, and two days in, my wife's father had a heart attack. I had to fly to California and drop out of the academy.

I was lucky enough to get my old job back in the interim, but I reapplied and went through the whole process again as soon as I could. It was about a year later, in early 2007, I was back at the academy. Now, fifteen years later, I don't regret one bit of it. From day one, I enjoyed putting the uniform on and still do. I'm one of those weird guys who has been in patrol for fifteen years, and I still love patrol cars. For me, that's the bread and butter of being a police officer and connecting with your community.

It wasn't always easy. Changing careers put my family in financial turmoil. I lost my house, and we lost all of our cars. But we've slowly rebuilt our lives. My biggest hero is my wife because she supported my decision and went through a considerable change in our lifestyle. Yet, she's always been supportive through all the financial and other challenges. I'm so grateful for her standing with me because I just love being a police officer. I love helping people, and I love arresting people. What I mean by that is that after I have to arrest someone, I want to make a connection with them. I want to know what's going on in their life and see if there's anything I can do to help them change their path. You know, a lot of times, it's not a good situation at the time of the arrest. Obviously, they don't like me because I'm taking them away from whatever they were doing and taking away their freedom. But it's the conversations you have from the place where you arrest them to the jail that can make a difference. And, yes, I've had people reach out to me. I've had successful stories, but even those that didn't turn out to be positive, I know I planted a seed in that person's life that might help them down the road.

We never know the impact we'll have on someone's life. And meeting Brandon Tatum was one of those great stories. I was sitting in my patrol car outside the station, just doing paperwork. I never did that before, but for some reason, there I was. I saw this vehicle pull up out of the corner of my eye. It's got giant rims, big tires, a little bit lifted. I think Brandon was wearing a do-rag, and he's all tatted up. I see him in this car, and the first thing in my mind was, *is this guy going to try to hurt me? What's about to happen?* I look at him, and he says, "Hey, I want to be a police officer. I need to know what I need to do to become a police officer." *Whew!* I started to relax a little bit, and we engaged in a good conversation. I was like, you know, dude, I'll take you on a ride-along so you can experience what it's like to be an officer. Of course, it ended up great, but that initial feeling was no joke—I was putting my hand on my gun. We did the ride-along pretty quickly, and I don't think he even got to ride with me through an entire shift but, to know that was the start of his career means a lot to me. To watch Brandon go from that moment to where he ended up in the police department and to see the success he's having is amazing. The best part of this experience was gaining a lifelong friend in Brandon.

Brandon and I even co-taught some classes on procedural justice and twenty-first century policing. It was a fun journey with Brandon, and I remember early on, we used to respectfully debate about things because, at that time, he had different political views than he does today. But even then, when we disagreed on certain things, I always respected him and his opinions. I know that people like to play up race, especially when they look at police officers, but I don't care about someone's race or whatever labels people want to put on others. My only perspective is that I'm a God-fearing man, and therefore, I love all people. I remember telling Brandon to always do his own research and do his own investigation. Don't just take what people say and go with that. Well, Brandon has the type of character that he does that. That's why he is where he is now. Not because of something I said, or someone else said, or because mainstream media said, but because he took the time to research it for himself.

These days, I don't even watch the news anymore. I haven't for about a year. I think much of the news has a bias toward their own agenda. Instead of giving just the facts and letting people decide independently, it seems they're leaning toward the left and toward a specific agenda. I think it's unfortunate and unfair to block people's social media because they don't like what they say. I know we don't all agree; even I can't entirely agree with everything the Right or the Left says. But it's not American to take away someone's voice. Everyone should have a platform where they can express their point of view. And the limiting of voices is definitely a part of what's dividing Americans.

When it comes to how police officers are portrayed, I feel like they get pleasure—and when I say *they*, I mean the media—and get satisfaction in projecting officers in a bad light. Officers do so many good things on a day-to-day basis, but you don't see that. I'm not naive enough to believe there are no bad cops. Good cops who work hard to do the right thing all the time don't like when those officers disgrace the badge. But I do know we're dealing with human beings, good ones and bad ones. We can all work hard and do the right thing and weed those bad people out. I think it would help a lot if they would report on the good things that officers do. If I see someone hurting or cold, I'll go to the store and buy that person a jacket, shoes, food, or whatever I can. There are a lot of good police officers out there doing things like that every day. But people don't even know that happens. It's frustrating to me this whole narrative that cops are racist. I think people believe because of the continuous bombardment of bad press. I'm in the Tucson area, so I can only speak to this community. But I think the amount of any racism on a police force is equal to the amount of racism in a given community. Cops are not inherently racist.

In fact, I think if there's any group of people that aren't racist, it would be cops. You can't do your job and help people if you are racist. If your true calling is to be a cop, serve, and help people, you have that in your heart. For cops, there are different ways you help people: you make arrests, you take away some of their pain, help lift them from whatever they're experiencing. You can also help by directing them towards a different path, providing available resources to help them eventually become contributing members of their community. But you aren't able to do your job, to help your community if you're racist. It breaks my heart when I hear all these attacks on cops. It cuts deep when I contact someone of a different race, and they accuse me of making contact with them based on their race. I admit that can make me defensive, but I try to let it roll off my shoulders and just be kind and continue to talk with them. I get that some people have had bad experiences with other police officers where that might have been true; I don't know, and that was not me. But this is the first time they're encountering me, and to immediately go right there, it's hard. I know they don't know me, and they're accusing me of something when they don't know my heart. They don't know that I've got three adult children who are black, and to me, it does not matter the color of their skin; they are just my beautiful children. I really want that whole mindset to change across the country, and so, when someone says something like that to me, I think, wow, we still have a lot of work to do. And then I think, it's not going to change anytime soon. And then I just get discouraged.

BACK TO BRANDON

Every officer and every story is unique. I'm sure you get that after hearing from Officer Lew, Officer Tillman, Officer Hamilton, Officer Minner, and Officer Payne. No matter how they became an officer, each one wears their uniform proudly with the goal of serving their community and keeping citizens safe. One of my goals is to help everyone who reads this book understand and remember that. The stories they share are just a few of many. There are countless officers who are struggling with the job, the career they feel is a calling. I know that the majority—the major majority—of cops do not see color when they put on the uniform. It doesn't matter if they're male, female, black, white, gay, straight, or any other identifier you want to throw out there. To police officers, they are a team, they are a squad, they are partners. So, when they hear people say all cops are racist, it hurts because it's a lie. When they hear that their community doesn't want them anymore, that's disheartening. But they still suit up every day and go out to serve. Cops are not perfect, but they are amazing heroes who sacrifice their own lives to protect yours.

Chapter Six:
DEFEND, NOT DEFUND

Y ou've just read some stories from police officers around the country about how hard it can be being a police officer. It's hard enough for anyone to have a job where you really don't know if you're coming home at the end of the night. With racial tensions at an all-time high, imagine having that job and being called a racist, not because of how you treat people but solely because of the uniform you wear. Now imagine adding into the mix that you're a black cop. There's no need to imagine—it's real. Can you believe that there are people who are so myopic that they believe all cops are racists? They even believe that black officers are racists. White people are actually shouting at black officers calling them racist. It's absolutely ridiculous!

I know a lot of politicians and citizens have shouted, screamed, and even rioted to spread support for the idea of "defunding the police" as the solution to every perceived wrong in our society and specifically, within the judicial system and the police department. They think that defunding the police will solve racism, or at least that's what they're trying to sell to the American public. Well, I wanna get real with everyone reading this book about what that really means and the likely results in communities and cities taking steps to do this. First, I want to talk about this alleged systemic racism on the force. Yes, alleged. Then I'll share the reality of defunding as one of the most misguided ideas ever.

Police Are the Least Racist People Out There

Before anyone freaks out, yes, I acknowledge and agree that there are some incidents where police officers overstep their bounds and use too much force, too much power. The media and the protesters on the street keep shouting that defunding the police is necessary because all of these cops—primarily white cops—commit too much violence against black men. They say the problem of systemic racism within the police force is the primary issue in communities, especially communities with high crime rates. I will lay it out for you right now—police are the least racist people I know. Yes, I said it.

Police officers are the least racist people, and I should know because I have been a police officer, and—in case you didn't notice the photo of me in the book or have never watched one of my videos—I am a black man. Always have been, always will be. Right now, it seems like I'm one of the only people who will keep it 100! I'm not afraid of what people will think or what people will do if I speak the truth. I have to speak out and stand up for my fellow brothers and sisters in blue. Most police officers don't have a voice. They can't say the stuff that I say, but they know what I'm saying is true. However, they risk being demonized and possibly fired if they say anything publicly. That's why I am speaking out for them. I'm gonna keep it real with y'all. I believe, and I'm gonna tell you why I believe that police officers are probably the least racist people in our society.

I will say it again in case anyone thinks I am living in denial. *Of course, we've got some cops on the police force who are racists.* If I am being 100, there are racist cops—you've got racist white cops, and you've got racist cops who are black and racist cops who are

Hispanic. Seriously, you've got people of all backgrounds who are racist or prejudiced in the police department—it's true. *However,* the fact is that those racist officers are not the majority; they are the minority. There are police departments with few to no racists on the force—as in none, zero. I'll tell you why I believe that. Let me throw some statistics in here really quick so we can get a better understanding, because a lot of people are falling through the cracks with statistics that are displayed out of context. Yes, it is true that police officers are patrolling African American communities at a disproportionate rate. Yes, it is true that black people get arrested at a disproportionate rate. Yes, it is true that disproportionately, black people are having force used against them and are getting into deadly conflicts with police officers. But here are the contextual stats that you need to know so you don't get brainwashed: African American people in this country commit a greater amount of crimes. According to the 2018 census, about 13 percent of the United Sates is black or African American.[4] And less than half of that 13 percent of the population are criminals—less than half (so less than 6 percent of the entire American population). However, less than 6 percent of black US citizens commit about half of the murders in this country. Did you get that? Over half of all violent crimes in this country are committed by less than 6 percent of the population in our country.

Are you ready for another shocker? These numbers only represent actual convictions. I'm not even talking about crimes committed where no one is arrested and convicted. Did you know that in Chicago, over 80 percent of violent crimes and shootings never get solved?[5] That's a whole criminal element that doesn't even get

---

4 Jason L. Riley, "Family Secret: What the Left Won't Tell You about Black Crime," *Washington Times*, July 21, 2014, https://www.washingtontimes.com/news/2014/jul/21/family-secret-what-the-left-wont-tell-you-about-bl/.

5 Chip Mitchell, "Chicago's Dismal Murder Solve Rate Even Worse When Victims Are Black," NPR, October 9, 2019, https://www.npr.org/local/309/2019/10/09/768552458/chicago-s-dismal-murder-solve-rate-even-worse-when-victims-are-black.

counted. So, you could add an even higher number of violent crimes like homicide being committed by mostly blacks. In large urban areas, most of the violent crime is due to gang violence and inner-city violence. Those are not even factored into the statistics I shared because no one is being convicted of those crimes. So, yeah, do the math. Of course, that's why black neighborhoods get patrolled disproportionately.

Another thing that people don't realize, or don't want to acknowledge, is that white people get killed by police nearly twice as often as black people, and nearly twice as many of them are unarmed victims. People like to brush that off and say it's because of the population number. Well, that's not true because cops don't patrol everybody in the United States of America. They only patrol the criminal element, the criminal neighborhoods. So, if you have a disproportionate group, which is the black group, committing more of the crimes, then white people aren't committing the same percentage of crime, but yet they're getting shot more than black people. All you have to do is do the math. They patrol black people at a disproportionate rate, but they kill white people twice as much. Really? This is not the narrative that people want to tell you about, but it's the myth that is projected in saying that white police officers are racist, or there's some type of systemic racism in the police department. Statistics show that it's just not true.

When I was an officer in the Tucson Police Department, remember, I held a variety of positions: I was a spokesperson for the department; I was on the SWAT team; I was a field training officer. That means I have worked in nearly every aspect of a police department. I helped train new officers coming into my division and taught at the academy as well. With all these roles, that meant I knew all about public records. I knew about internal affairs. I knew which police officers were getting fired, and I knew which ones were getting hired. I've worked in plenty of divisions with detectives—all of that. And in all that time, with all that exposure to new and existing officers, from rookies to top-ranking detectives, never once did I come across a racist cop. Never. Even if there was a cop who was racist on the inside, it was never portrayed or never projected.

I think it's important to say again—I never came across a racist police officer. And there was a clear reason why. First of all, nobody likes racist people—nobody. So, it's a very unpopular stance. And in policing specifically, racism is not an effective way to do your job. If you are sitting around wasting your time pulling over black people just because of the color of their skin, you're not going to progress within the department. Oh, by the way, here's a fun fact: in most cases, when you're pulling somebody over in traffic, you don't even know what race they are. I'm serious. All you have to do is drive down the street in your car today during the daytime, and you pull up behind someone and tell me what race they are from behind them. In about 99 percent of the cases, you won't know. Anyway, for police officers, it's of no benefit to spin your wheels by pulling over just black people. Especially if they don't have drugs or are not committing crimes. It's wasted time on a useless activity, and the officer is not going to get any recognition or build a positive reputation. When most police officers join the force, they have a strong desire to get onto and work in a specialty unit. In order to do that, they need a record—a résumé if you want to call it that—built on making valid arrests and doing effective policing. Making useless traffic stops will not help officers get into any special units.

To develop a good reputation, an officer needs to make valid arrests and that often equates with drug arrests. The more valid drug arrests made, the better a cop's record, right? And, in case you didn't know, every race sells drugs. You can pick your poison, but drug crimes are not limited to any specific race. That means white people sell drugs, black people sell drugs, Hispanic people sell drugs, Asian people sell drugs. You get the idea? So, for an officer to just identify one race means they're missing all these other drug crimes out there. It's common sense to broaden your net, and most officers have a lot of common sense. They're looking to make arrests for people selling meth, selling heroin, selling crack, and selling fentanyl. When they do that, they end up with all these arrests because they aren't looking at the race, they're looking at behaviors. They're looking at trends, so they're over here winning. But this fictionalized racist cop that the media and politicians talk about would be over on the other side losing because they're trying to be racist. It's not beneficial to an officer's career track, and that's one reason police are the least racist people out there.

Now let's talk about the white police officer in the black community, because I think that type of police officer is the least racist of the least racist. Think about this for a minute. The issue with most folks is that they watch too much TV and make decisions based on that. These folks just imagine what cops do on a day-to-day basis but have no idea what's going on. Cops who work in black communities—they get two things, two types of exposure, that I think are invaluable to the argument I'm making. One is they have access, experience, and exposure to all kinds of black people. In these communities, everybody is not a criminal. Everybody's not a stereotypical ghetto *Ray-Ray*[6] running around with a shotgun or a stolen handgun in his pocket selling crack on the corner. That's not the totality of the community. Even if that 6 percent of the population is criminal, that's still only a portion of the community that terrorizes everybody else. As police officers in these communities, they get to meet and serve the other part of the community. They get to talk to a grandma who's been victimized. They talk to young kids who have been victimized. They talk to the mom who has to put her child in a casket because of gun violence. Cops in these communities have exposure to all types of people. People who are making money, people who are wealthy,

6 Ray-ray, Urban Dictionary, https://www.urbandictionary.com/define.php?term=ray-ray.

people who are upstanding citizens, and believe it or not, even some black people who want to be police officers, who aspire to be in the military, who love this country.

Police officers get a plethora or wide range of exposure to a number of good people, and then they get the bad apples in the neighborhood as well. But no matter what, these cops are putting their life on the line for all these black people. They are willing to lose their life, lose their future for black folks. You're hearing about all these racist white people out there running rampant. But I'm telling you that these people are willing to put their own life on the line for black people. In fact, black or white, when people become police officers, they sign up for this service and are willing to put their own life on the line for their own citizens—for their own community. Least racist people, are you beginning to hear me?

When officers spend a lot of time patrolling the same community, they build up a tolerance for violence that people who are not patrolling these black communities do not build up. Now, tolerance does not mean complacency. It's just that what they see on a day-to-day basis—the violence, the investigations, the activities—they are no longer shocked. They understand the community they police and have learned how to cope with policing in a balanced way in these communities. That balance, that ability to keep coming back day after day, may be misunderstood as callous, but it is so far from the truth. They show up every day to protect the residents of that community. That commitment to never-ending service can in no way be called racism.

I get it that there are people out there saying police officers are targeting black people, but when you understand a bit more about how police are assigned, you'll see the truth. Police officers are not assigned to one generic precinct that covers the entire city. They are assigned to specific precincts in different parts of the city. They equally disperse cops in certain divisions in order to accomplish coverage for the entire city. So, if officers are assigned to the north side of a city, that's where they work. They don't just randomly patrol in another area. They don't drive into another area so they can target any specific person or race. It doesn't work like that. You police, support, protect, and serve the district or area you're assigned to. Cops don't pick and choose either; they accept the area that's assigned to them. If a cop works in the north and the north is primarily white, then they're naturally going to be dealing with white folks because that's who lives there. And it doesn't matter if the officers are black, white, Asian, or Hispanic, cops are not assigned to a precinct or division based on their color. So, that means that, yes, it is possible that you will have white cops in a community that is mostly black citizens. If those cops are doing their job, who do you think they're gonna stop? Who else do you think they're gonna arrest when a crime is committed? Who? They only have one choice. And that's the people who live in that community.

Not only is there little to no racism among cops when dealing with the community, but there is also even less, if any, racism among police officers. Being a police officer is not an easy job, and you have to be a special person to even sign up to work in a police department. So, hear me when I say that even the lowest of the low in the police department are average to decent human beings by regular standards. That's just my personal opinion. I knew officers who were rude, who had a poor attitude, people I wouldn't even want to invite to my house to eat dinner. But let me say this loud and clear, I have witnessed those same rude cops with bad attitudes save, I don't know, ten to fifteen people's lives. I have personally witnessed them put their life on the line for other people. Some of them got shot to protect a single mom, and some of them got shot to protect a crackhead. So even the ones down at the bottom of the personality rating, even those who have a terrible reputation in the department, have saved more lives than the average person in America. Even they have contributed to the success of more people than a lot of people in America. I'm just keeping it 100.

Don't get me wrong: I don't condone police officers not having great attitudes, but I know people are human. And in case you were wondering, it isn't in the *serve and protect* oath that one has to be sweet and kind and touchy-feely with people. That's just not the way it works. I think there are a lot of misconceptions out there. There's a lot of perspective that needs to be had no matter what race you are. If you're a police officer, you're going through a lot. You're putting it all on the line every day you're on the job. You're willing to sacrifice it all, and you've seen stuff that nobody else has been able to see and nobody else wants to see, and probably couldn't even survive after seeing some of the stuff. Along with being in situations that most people can't survive in, another thing I want people to understand is the camaraderie between police officers. At least in my department and a few other departments that I know of—there's not racism going on within the department. You know you got these SJWs who want to think everything is racist, but there's no racism going on in the department. It's like a football team or the military—we're all on the same team. We all put on the badge the same way. We all would do anything for one another. My white partners in the police department would take a bullet for me just as fast as anybody else.

Let me share a personal story with you. This is an ideal example of what I experienced on the police force. I want to share this specific story because I think if people knew that this story—my story—is not unique, folks would realize they don't really know about policing. My hope is that everyone who reads this story will walk away with a different perspective.

One of my good friends—and we're really close friends now because of what he did—was on a call for service with me. When I showed up, I saw a guy who had a swastika on his forehead. He was a white nationalist or something, and he didn't want a black officer taking his call for service. Now, realize we, as officers, don't get to choose the calls we respond to, and the people who call for service don't get to choose who comes.

They get who shows up. So, I get there, and he's on the phone saying, "I don't want no black man taking a police report from me. I only want the white guy to take it." Well, that's when my friend and partner stepped up in a big way. He ripped this guy's you know what. I mean, he got on him. He said, "You better not ever say something like that to me ever again. We'll leave. We won't serve you!" He just went on and was ripping that guy down. BOOM! BOOM! BOOM! And I'm looking at him like...DANG! He really had my back, and I really got that. I understood. You know what I'm saying? He told that guy he could not say something like that about his partner. He stood up for me in a big way, a vocal way, a visible way. From that point on, I respected him even more than I did before. A lot of cops are too afraid to get into that battle on duty, but he went hard for me. And he was a young officer, still making his reputation. I guarantee you that this happens in police departments all over the country. There are multiple races in a police department, and we're all one team, one family, willing to die for one another even when we bicker and disagree. We're still willing to go that extra mile. I hope this gives people some insight into policing in America, into the idea of racist cops in America. It's just not the case.

Defunding the Police Will Backfire

I hope you understood what I said about the lack of racism on the police force. Now I'd like to talk about what defunding the police will actually do to the communities. Most people who say they support defunding the police don't really have any idea what they're talking about—no idea. I'll say it again: they have no idea what that means! The core of this shouting for defunding is because too many people don't appreciate the police. They just want to eliminate millions and millions of dollars from police department budgets around the country. And when you defund the police department, you know what that means, right? Don't listen to all those who are lying about what it means to defund the police department. What are you defunding? You know they're gonna go for the pay. You know they're gonna go for the pensions. You know they're gonna dip into that retirement. And you know they're gonna make every police force smaller, with fewer officers doing the same work. People act like defunding the police isn't a big deal. Oh, they say they're just redirecting and diverting responsibilities to other places. No. They are dismantling the core structure of the police department.

Like I said, there are too many people who don't appreciate the police and what they do in your communities. Too many people actually hate the police officers because they're listening to false narratives instead of the truth. They don't care anything about your life; they don't care. It's about votes. It's about political correctness. It's about the long game of running our country in order to create something new. They want to create some kind of utopia based on a concept that has never worked in the history of the world. Socialism and communism don't work. Some people would have you believe that reducing the police force is step one toward this utopia, but it's step one toward real chaos.

Some of you, or people you know, believe that cops don't need to be involved with some of the responsibilities they currently have. I won't lie to you—police officers have a lot of duties, and they could use some help. But there's the argument out there that community citizens can do a better job than officers when it comes to things like domestic violence and mental health situations. Do you really want to take police from single moms? Vulnerable children? Domestic violence victims? The people who need police officers the most. That's robbing them of the protection they deserve, and anyone who believes that should be ashamed of themselves. Well, let's talk about those things. Let's talk about what it will really be like without cops. Here's another reality check.

You need to know there are dangerous, evil people in this world. It's just a fact. That's not something I take pleasure in saying, but it is a reality. We have to start with that fact on the table. And when a dangerous, evil person comes to your front door and forces entry into your house, with your children there, who are you gonna call? Not the activists who are out in the streets protesting to defund the police. Not the politicians who supported those protests and then voted to cut the police budget in half. They will not be there for you. You're gonna call a man or a woman who's sworn to uphold the law wearing a badge. These people do not cower from danger. They won't turn away from you because of your race or because of what you look like or because of your past mistakes. They will come into your house and protect you with their life. No matter what the consequences are, and hear this: no matter if they never come home to see their own family, they will be there for you and yours. And at that time, probably the most frightening time in your life, you will be glad they are there. You will be glad they answered the call.

You do realize that cops do not do their job for the money, right? When I was an officer, I made $50,000 a year. Clearly, I didn't do it for the money. I did it because I loved my community. You couldn't pay me enough to put my life on the line. You couldn't pay me enough to worry about not coming home every night to my children. So, when it comes to defunding the police, realize it's people who do their job to serve others that you're talking about defunding. I believe that the people who are behind this idea owe it to America to explain what part of the police department they plan on cutting. Who doesn't deserve the service and protection of the police? Will they cut the domestic violence unit? Will they cut the individuals who investigate child sex crimes? Internet crimes? Elder abuse? How about cutting the SWAT team—who, by the way, are some of the best-trained men and women in the entire world? Who do you think is gonna handle terrorist attacks on American soil? Who do you think is gonna stop the drug dealers from dealing drugs to your children? Who's gonna do that for you? Everyday citizens and social workers are not equipped to do that. That's why you have police officers who go through the training.

Most people have never been to a police academy. They don't know what cops learn or understand the sacrifices that are made. People say that officers are not well trained without knowing how much time is spent learning about the laws and learning about the Constitution. There is also a great deal of time spent learning about how to de-escalate situations, crisis intervention, and mental health crises. Officers also learn how to drive and how to shoot. That includes when to shoot, why to shoot, and where to shoot. These days, people want to just shout out how bad cops are and how everything race-related is their fault. You know what? It's the fault of people like them that others are out there ambushing and killing police officers for no reason. There is a real, palpable hatred and vitriol for really good people. There is now a deep animosity that should not exist. For anyone who thinks about hating the police and publicizing that hatred, you need to understand that you're putting a target on their backs. You're making it unsafe for them to go to work. What do you think you're doing to the morale? Do you think it's exciting for a police officer to go to work?

Who wants to work in an environment where you're not wanted? Who wants to work for a city council that doesn't support you? Who wants to work for people who don't care if you die? That's why you have cases of the "blue flu" in so many police departments. For those of you who don't know what blue flu is, that's when police officers call in sick in unprecedented numbers. Because the thing is, departments can monitor, measure, and even deny or delay your vacation leave, but they can't tell you when you can call in sick. At least not for that one day, no one can ask you any questions about your illness if you call in sick. It's often the only way they can voice their opinion without retribution.

Police officers have called in sick all around the country—deservedly so, deservedly so. That's why three hundred officers didn't show up on the Fourth of July weekend 2020. It was a historic homicidal weekend in LA. Historic! But they didn't have the support of their city, so they had to send a message the best way they could. Why does that send a message? Please, people, put two and two together. When you don't have police, you have crime, you have death, you have destruction. You have dismay. Your community is ruined. Get it through your skull. Do not listen to the politicians and social justice warriors who are selling you a false narrative about your safety. Remember, they don't care how well you sleep at night. They don't care if you're now scared to walk to your car or across the street for a gallon of milk. They don't care about the individual, as long as they can make their political point.

And, as much as I loved being a police officer, I have enough respect for the uniform and the job officers do to say I'm glad these police officers are exercising the blue flu. And I pray to God that all around the country, every place where they're defunding the police, that officers just call in sick or move laterally or retire. Listen, I don't wish for violence or destruction. I want communities to be safe and livable for their citizens. But I want those cities to wake up. I want the citizens challenging the city council that thinks it's a good idea to defund the police, especially if the police are showing you that you need them. Maybe these communities should be destroyed so folks will understand that we cannot have peace in our streets without police officers. Do you hear me? I wish that people in the communities promoting defunding the police would go down to the city council and use that same energy protesting against racism and against capitalism to protest in support of these police officers. And, if your community, your city, won't provide you safety and protection via a well-funded police force, then I support you moving somewhere else.

If anyone out there reading this book still thinks cops are the problem and that we just need to do away with the police officer, then please do not ever call the police. Why should someone risk their life for you if you just want to throw them under the bus? I know that in some cities, they have called for and already removed School Resources Officers. Cities are actually removing police officers who believe their number-one job is to protect the lives of students and faculty. If you think that's okay and they don't matter, then when somebody comes into the school bussin,[7] don't call the police. Don't call the freakin' police. Somebody comes in that school bussin, I want whatever resource y'all created outside of law enforcement to take care of the situation. Don't call the police. Good officers shouldn't even be putting their lives on the line and going into a dangerous situation like that. Don't call the police. You wanna take resource officers out of the school, then don't ask them to be there when trouble shows up. When a big ol' gang fight breaks out at the school, don't ask the police to make any arrests. If a teacher assaults one of these kids, don't call the police. Why don't you call the mayor to do the investigation? Don't call the police, because when you're pulling officers out of schools and saying we don't want your help, your protection, then you're saying a big F-U to the police officers. It's like refusing to pay your insurance premium but expecting your insurance company to still step in and pay you when your house burns down or whatever. It just doesn't make sense. You have no real reason to do that because SROs do not bring problems to schools—they prevent them. But this type of defunding and removal is nothing but an FU to the officers and police department. It's the community saying we don't need you and we don't want you. Well, if you think this is a good idea, then when stuff hits the fan at your school, don't call the police.

I get it that there are people who believe they don't need the police and then don't want them in their neighborhoods. I wish those people could exempt themselves from being on a 911 call. They should be able to say, *I'm exempt*. They should not have

---

7 Bussin, Urban Dictionary, https://www.urbandictionary.com/define.php?term=bussin.

to pay taxes that support the police department. They should be exempt. However, that also means when somebody comes to their house, they can't call 911. They should get a busy signal because their addresses, their numbers have been blocked from service. Now, do I really wish harm on people? Absolutely not. But I wish that we could do that because I guarantee you the first time that person, that household, needs the police and they're not there, that attitude will change. The first time some criminal runs into their house and decides to duct-tape them into submission and rob them, what do you think that homeowner wants to do? They want to call the police. They'll want to be saved and protected. They'll want that criminal arrested, and they'll want justice. Seriously, if people who don't want the police could not call the police, then cops' jobs would be a lot easier.

But that's not reality. The reality is much closer to a quote that has been inaccurately credited to George Orwell. And although he didn't actually say it, he did say something similar in a couple of his essays. And it was used perfectly in the film *Crown Vic*. At the end of a very rough day, a training officer says to the rookie cop questioning his career choice after his first night of patrol, "People sleep peaceably in their beds at night only because rough men stand ready to do violence on their behalf." Then the training officers adds, "And they will hate us for it."

Can you imagine why anybody would want to be a police officer right now? Why? You see, not only are people leaving the police force, but there are also fewer people signing up to serve. In fact, in some cities, the funding for training new officers has been removed from the budget. Who would want to have a job where the media paints you in a negative light and too many people seem to despise you? Again, I ask, can you imagine why anybody would want to be a police officer right now?

But here's the crazy thing—there are so many good men and women who still want to become police officers. They've had a passion since the day they were born to be a servant to their community. I want you to understand this: policing in America is not just a job—it's a calling. And there are people who answer the call on a day-to-day basis. Despite so many out there trying to destroy their dream of serving their communities, they're still trying.

There are a few more facts I need to share with you about why the entire defund the police movement is based on a farce. It's being done for political gain and nothing more. Sure, there are some people who have legitimate complaints and concerns about police using excessive force. But I will tell you that it's not based on race, as I've already explained. Now, I want to talk to you about some of the loudest voices screaming to defund police departments.

Are you ready for this? The loudest voices and those getting the most press time on mainstream media are politicians and celebrities. They are yelling at you, telling you that you should defund the police. They are fraudulent! While they're screaming to defund police and do away with officers, guess what they have? Armed security. People who are there to protect them twenty-four hours a day. They have guns. You don't. And it breaks my heart to see men and women of integrity, amazing police officers, lose their lives protecting others, and the community is silent. One horrific example is the retired police captain, David Dorn, who honorably served in the police department for thirty-eight years and was a well-respected community leader. He was helping protect a privately owned place of business when he was shot and killed during a looting. It was even recorded on a live stream on social media. And what was said? Nothing! Nothing! There was no outrage or protest for him.

People should be thinking about defunding the criminal element in the community. Too many people are focused on the wrong area. We all understand policing, and I think every officer out there knows things can be improved. I would love to see police officers have the ability to have more training and more support with certain situations. Guess what? That comes with more funding, not defunding.

Let me tell you what needs to be defunded: these failed government programs that have done nothing for young people in the inner city. Let's get rid of frivolous programs that have not provided opportunities or education for our young people. They have done nothing for the communities. The proper funding of the police department is where you see success. A well-funded police department with good, adequate training, that's what's going to protect the young people. That's what's gonna keep people safe. That's what's gonna get the guns off the streets. That's gonna give young people an opportunity to flourish, to live their dreams, to accomplish things without getting snuffed out through gang violence, through drugs, through homicides. It's common sense! But, y'all, there are too many people who are not operating on common sense. They're operating on emotions. They're operating on political correctness. They're operating on mob rule. You and I both know what's really going on in these cities. You and I both know that the politicians have failed you. You and I know that you're not really worried that a police offi-cer cruising down your street might harass you. You're worried about wearing the wrong color on the wrong street. You're wor-ried about the dope boys in the hood selling dope, creating zom-bies. And for you hypocrites out there, you should be ashamed of yourselves. Because you know you're doing this for political expediency. You're doing this for elections. You know you really don't care about the inner city. You really don't care about vio-lence, because if you did, you would have done something about this thirty or forty years ago.

Let me talk to you about what will happen, what gets cut from the police department when you defund them. Are you going to be there to protect women from getting abused? Are you gonna be there for children who are on the internet getting exposed to predators? Are you gonna be there when a woman is giving birth on the side of the road? Are you gonna be there when someone is lying in the middle of the street with gunshot wounds? I need you to wake up! Use your brain. The police officers who go on patrol through your communities are out there to serve and protect every day. They deserve support. They deserve funding. They deserve to be trained properly. They deserve to have the backing of the city. You're gonna take police from single moms, vulnerable children, domestic violence victims? These are the people who need them the most. You're robbing them, and people who think this is a viable solution, an answer for the inner cities? They should be ashamed. There are bad apples in every profession; the police department is not exempt. And every single person I've talked to, every single person watching videos of police violence, they all hate bad cops. But you know who hates bad cops the most? The good cops! The ones who stick around. The ones who serve properly. And you're making it hard on them. Patriotic Americans don't defund the police; they defend the police. I hope you're getting the message that we need to back the blue. I hope you'll join me and others in supporting police officers all over the country so we can make this country a better place.

Social Workers vs. Real Police

I said I wanted to share the reasons that defunding the police is one of the most misguided ideas out there. So, point number one is that police are the least racist people in any given community. Point number two is that defunding the police just takes away vital protection from those most in need. Now, point number three is to take a look at social workers versus real police officers. Before I go further, I will say that social workers are amazing people who also choose their careers as a way to serve the community. That's a fact. However, it's also a fact that they are trained differently than officers. Still, there are people out there saying social workers should be called in rather than police officers on certain types of incidents. Let me share with you what the facts are if that happens.

Let's start with the idea that you want to send a social worker to a domestic violence call. People, the politicians who are out there telling you this is a good idea are selling you a dream. As a matter of fact, they're selling you a nightmare! They're telling you that it makes sense to defund the police department, which means they will cut back on resources for police officers—real police officers—they will cut back on staffing, and instead hire and give money to a citizen response unit. Whatever they want to call it. Freedom fighters—I think in Minneapolis, they call them freedom fighters. They want citizens to go to these calls. The people pushing this narrative are saying that police officers don't need to go to mental health calls. Police officers shouldn't go to domestic violence calls. I'm like, bra' what?! I just don't understand how they can believe this. I mean, my son—a nine-year-old boy— probably understands that you can't just send a social worker to these potentially violent calls. Let me give you an example of why. When I was a police officer, I had to go on more than one domestic violence call. So, let me share with you an example of what's likely to happen.

You send a social worker to a domestic violence call. I'm going to assume that you're not going to have them go through a year of training like police officers are required to complete. They're not going to have to learn de-escalation tactics. I'm talking about in tactical situations, not just de-escalating somebody sitting on the couch being calm. I'm talking about de-escalating somebody who has now gone into a manic state, and they're ready to choke you out. So, de-escalation, learning defensive tactics—meaning learning how to fight—they're not going to have that specific training. So, they walk into that situation, and you expect them to remain poised under pressure, but what happens when that person starts kicking that social worker in the head? Are they going to be trained for all this? They will also need to know Constitutional rights, they need to know laws, they have to know all this stuff before they can go into your house. What they can and cannot do according to the law. Too many people think you can just reason with someone in a violent rage, and it doesn't work that way. Remember, even if someone figures out that social workers need special training, that community wants to replace the police officers right now. That means they start out untrained.

That social worker is walking into a domestic violence situation. Domestic violence (or DV) calls are the most dangerous calls a police officer can ever go to because they're emotionally driven, and people will crack up on you in a split second. They're going to go to a call where a woman got beaten up by her boyfriend. These brain-dead politicians are assuming that baby daddy is going to flee from the house, and say, "I'll never go back to that house again. You know? Because the police aren't there, and I don't want to go and scare that social worker." They want you to believe he's never going to come back to the house. However, in reality, you've got the social worker in there, the girlfriend gets all crazy, she's crying. He comes back because he's ready to wipe the whole house out. And you've got the poor old social worker in there who hasn't ever been in a stressful situation in their life. They're about to get bludgeoned because that violent boyfriend sees them as the enemy. Now you've got two or three victims in a situation where there should have been none.

You should do it like we did it in my police department— the REAL cops show up with training and experience. And if the stuff hits the fan, they can deal with it. And then once the police officers get the situation under control, or they stand guard outside, then—and only then—should you have the social worker come in and whisper sweet nothings into their ear. But until then, you need real police with real tactics.

I'm not making this up. There was a very recent case where an officer showed up at a residence for a DV call. It started out as a peaceful environment. The young lady was happy to see the officers, and she was there to collect her belongings to leave the premises. The on-site officers were there to assist her. The abuser, the man in the incident, is gone. He is not there, so this is now a safe environment. This is definitely a place where a social worker could come in and talk to her. Right? She can get the help she needs, and everything is going to be okay.

There is video footage of this situation because of bodycams, so I'm not making up what's about to happen and how quickly things can escalate. The officers already did a safety check and confirmed the man was not there. The woman didn't know about a gun and thought there might be something in a safe upstairs, but again, he's not there. Now, these officers did a fairly good job in checking out the home. However, they should never have their back to an open door. They need to be prepared if the perpetrator comes back. I learned to always have both officers in view of the front door or to close and lock that door to secure the area. This is what we learn if you end up, if you're in somebody's house, you want to shut and secure the door, in case he comes, so you'll have enough time to react if you need to. That's just my little side note.

Okay, so back to what happened. She's just confirmed again that he was gone, but that he would be coming back. They're talking to her about going to her sister's or getting a locksmith to change the locks. She looked up and said, "He's coming. He's coming." BAM! This guy comes blasting out of nowhere, through the front door and firing a gun.

It happened so fast that even watching the video, it's hard to grasp it. But these officers are shot! Now, my understanding is that these two officers survived, but they were definitely shot. And this is the type of thing that goes on in policing every day. And people want to send a social worker into situations like that? People criticize cops, and they say all these crazy things about police officers. But you know most people would never put themselves in a position that could end up like this, they would never do it. They will cower or back down. They will never do it. I want this to be clear.

This is why people like me, and others are saying, think about what your politicians are saying to you. If you were to defund the police. Police would not show up to this call. And if they weren't there to defend this lady, she would be dead. This young woman, instead of planning to go to her sister's, would be having a meeting with the Lord. Oh, and if those two officers had been social workers instead? They would be dead too. Look, the armed officers got shot, so there's no way a sweet, helpful social worker would stand a chance. But these guys risked it all. They took the risk that they might never go home see their family, just to protect this young lady for a few minutes.

I think that there's not enough of these stories out there where are describing police incidents and explaining what's going on so people can have a clear vivid picture of policing in America. This is just one example of why you need to tell a police officer, thank you for your service, and give them some respect, because they go through this stuff on a day-to-day basis, and they don't even complain about it.

Now, what about the mental health call? There are a lot of voices saying that social workers should be first on the scene here as well. Okay, so you've got a social worker going to a situation where a person is having a mental issue. I'm not saying this in a bad way, but sometimes people crack up; they have PTSD or whatever the case may be. Trust me, I've seen a lot of it. They go to that call. The residents (who may have even made the call themselves) don't tell them there's a firearm in the house, nothing like that. They just ask for the social worker to come over to the house and talk to that person who's having a mental health crisis. That person decides that they're gonna get wicked and end it all. As soon as the social worker shows up, they get a you-know-what (that's a gun, people) from the closet or the dresser or the safe or whatever, and they go and put that gun to their head and now they want to end it all. While the social worker is sitting there. What will that social worker do? Call the police?

Man, listen, listen—it's out of control, ladies and gentlemen; it's out of control. If you know anything about policing, there are things police officers should be there for. If you ask me, I think police officers should be there in all these situations, and you can have these social workers come in after the police. But it will not end well because these people have no idea what they're dealing with, and the folks yammering for defunding don't have a clue what they're talking about. They've never been a cop. They've never done a ride-along. They know nothing—nothing—about policing. And they're putting their cities, and in some cases their states, in critical condition. They're putting them in a position where they're literally in a backyard with a pit bull that hasn't eaten in a week and that's been fighting its whole life—that's what they're doing with these social workers. The people who think they know better will put them out there and let them get torn up.

Did I mention the legal ramifications of removing the police from these scenarios? There are going to be a tremendous number of lawsuits when it comes to social workers taking the position of a police officer. If at any point you violate somebody's rights, you get into a physical altercation with somebody, you are negligent, or you're not capable of defending them the way they should be defended, they will sue the mess out of the state, they'll sue the police department, and they're gonna sue the city council. The city is going to end up paying out lawsuits like nobody's business. Because if you get attacked as a social worker, you have to defend yourself, right? Or do you think you will just sit there until the police get there, which can take three minutes—or more? So, the social worker defends themselves, and they end up hurting somebody. They are then likely to be sued. But the folks out there demanding to defund the police aren't thinking about any of that. Instead, these misguided folks want to coddle your feelings and paint a picture of this community resource group fixing all the problems. The reality is they are going to coddle you straight to your demise.

Every coin has two sides, but this approach makes both sides bad. On side one is the kid who acts up but is never disciplined. They never get punished or spanked or whatever. There are no consequences, so they just play with your emotions and play with your emotions. Yet nothing ever happens to them. They get put into a corner to think about what they've done, and all they're thinking about is how they're gonna hurt you when they get out of the corner. Then they get out of the corner and do more bad stuff. That's what happens when people do not have to face consequences from bad choices. They will continue to make those bad choices, and probably worse choices, throughout their lives. Those are the people who have rioted, looted, hurt other citizens and police officers, and yet are not held accountable for the criminal element of their behavior. They learn that they can do whatever they want, damage whatever they want, and it's okay because it's expressing how they feel.

The other side of the coin is the community members, the social justice warriors, and the politicians who are making you believe they can address these real issues without police officers. They somehow believe that if there are no cops, the violence will magically stop. They believe that if social workers talk to domestic abusers, they'll see the error of their ways and just stop hitting their family members. They believe if they defund the police that peace will magically wash down the streets, and life will be all unicorns and rainbows.

The fact is that this coin, no matter which side you view, brings more chaos, more crime, and more violence to the streets— to your streets. Don't believe the lie that as long as you agree with those people, allowing and condoning the violence and anti-police messaging, things will get better. There have been too many examples of the angry mob turning on the very people who claim to support them. Windows were smashed in businesses showing pro-BLM signs. Small, minority-owned businesses have been ruined by mobs who say they support minorities. Crowds have turned on politicians who allowed violence because they didn't agree in lockstep with what the mob said they wanted. And, in case you haven't noticed, what the mob wants changes constantly because they will never be satisfied.

Chapter Seven:
HOPE STILL RISES

It sounds dark, doesn't it? It seems like there is no way to forge a better relationship between cops and communities. It might feel like law and order are out of reach, and there's no way to fight racism. Well, this black ex-officer can still see hope.

I believe that there is a way to bridge that great divide, to humanize us all, and to allow a way for everyone to think for themselves. Too much of this animosity is based on false information that keeps being repeated—repeated so much that too many people take it as truth, don't question the narrative, and become, as many say, *sheeple*! One of the reasons I speak out and continue to create my videos is to be one of the individual voices. I don't believe we have to follow the crowd. I will continue to be a voice and speak for conservative blacks and especially police officers, who don't have the voice they deserve these days. You should do the same. Stand up for officers and encourage them when you see them out. You have no idea how good it feels when a citizen says, "Thank you for your service." It can make all the difference in that officer's day. Change an officer's mind from wanting to give up to deciding to take one more call with the hope that humanity is redeemable. Send officers thank-you letters to the police department. If you get pulled over, and you were in the wrong, but the officers are reasonable, be kind. Encourage those you know who love policing to join the force. Support them. Teach your children to respect and appreciate law enforcement. Lastly, do more ride-alongs. Be informed and confident that your officers are out doing the right thing.

I'm not the only one who sees hope either. Those same officers who shared their struggles earlier in the book also have hopeful, positive experiences and ideas.

Changing the Narrative? –
More from Officer Lew

I believe ongoing, open discussion is the way to deal with this onslaught of negativity. While I don't want to force my opinions on people, there has to be an open discussion. I am hopeful that I see more people of influence speaking out; people like Brandon Tatum, Candace Owens, and Larry Elder, just to name a few. These influencers are waking people up, and that's a good thing!

There is a definite impact when more voices, more people speak out. My opinion is when you hear these messages about thinking for yourself, about embracing what you truly believe, not just what you've been told to believe, about standing up for yourself, it forces us to be held accountable. We may not like it, but that's got to change, and that's why it's hard to have that discussion. If we have that talk, we will eventually be in a better position as a people. We can change the victim mindset, and so much good will come from it. We grow up as young black people, and we always think everyone is against us. We learn that from our parents, and their parents, and far too many previous generations. We hear it in school as well. We get this false message that we're less than or beneath others. If we believe we're less than others, we're going to continue to be treated worse than others. And while it is multigenerational, I'm not teaching my kids that victim mentality.

I feel this new message is empowering and hopeful. These last five years have been a big wake-up process for me. I feel so empowered and at peace. Growing up, I was at a predominantly white school, only about 15 percent black. I remember getting the message that if you get good grades, you ain't black. If you're not getting in fights, you ain't black. If you don't play basketball, you ain't black. You have to do these things to fit in, or you have to be the class clown. I felt like I had to be the class clown. It's crazy that to fit in, you have to be the worst of the worst—be a criminal, get in fights, or do drugs. It's like we only have one culture in the African American community. White people don't have to be any certain way, so why is it that way with African Americans? Why is our culture negative? The expectations are low, negative, and bad. That whole mindset is bad, and I feel it starts at a young age.

I think that school resource officers can have a positive impact on young people. We as a country need to speak out about having them continue in the school systems and making sure that they are allowed to be armed—for their own safety, of course, but mostly so they can better protect students. We do live amid violence, and someone needs to be armed and at the ready. When kids see positive examples of police officers, it will work to change that negative narrative.

Another way to get the message out is through social media. It allows people to change that negative narrative easily just by posting a positive message. I use my social media page as a platform, and I get a lot of positive messages in my inbox that people love what I'm saying. However, as an active police officer, I can only speak so much and share so much of my opinion. It's not really because of any backlash or concerns from my department, but there is the reality of haters and the cancel culture. I push the line as much as I can, and I already hear comments like I'm an Uncle Tom or a coon or a sellout. I'm also concerned for my safety because there are some people out there who think crazy things. Someone could decide to get me fired or threaten me. It's happened with others, so I just have to be careful. That being said,

I'm not going to stop sharing my message. I am encouraged and think we're off to a great start with more vocal black conservatives. It will take time, but this is about to be a movement for good.

Reaching Out to the Young – More from Officer Ray Hamilton

I was so excited in early 2020 because I was selected to be an SRO. Due to COVID-19, everything has been put on hold. However, I'm ready to serve. I love children, and I have four of my own. My main focus is on the youth. I'm always looking to provide a positive experience. I realize that what they see and hear in music and on the news influences them. Unfortunately, it's often negative, and I want to overcome that. I don't want to add to that. I want to be the reason that a young person may believe something negative about police in general, but they will also say something like, *But that police officer I met—he's fair.*

I recently went through that very situation. I got called to talk to a young guy who was hanging out by a bank ATM. He looked a little raggedy, and because there had been a robbery over there a few days before, someone was worried. So, they called in and gave a description. I went there, saw the guy, and very casually got out of my car and approached him.

"Hey, man, can I talk to you really quick? I got a description of someone that looks just like you, and he was hanging out over by the bank ATM. Can I ask you a few questions?"

He said, "Yes."

I asked him why he was hanging out at the ATM, and he replied, "I just had an interview at the bank."

Well, that made sense to me, and I was just about to cut him loose. Then another guy rolls up on me. The way he's dressed, he looks like full-on Antifa—all dressed in black. He got out of his car and started aggressively walking toward me. I backed up a few steps and said, "Hey, what's going on?"

He starts yelling, "Why do you get to stop your car in the street and block traffic?"

Are you serious? I thought. I wondered if this might turn into something. So, I backed away from him a bit and radioed in what was happening. Then, I explained that the reason I'm blocking the street is that I stopped a guy that fit a description where a robbery had occurred. He was hanging out near the ATM, and somebody wanted me to talk to him. So that's what I was doing.

He just looked at me and said, "Oh."

Then, the guy I stopped—he's the one who defended me. He said, "Dude, leave him alone; he's just doing his job." That felt great. I showed him respect, and he returned it. *And* I also overcame that guy, and he apologized to me. He said he saw a lot of officers do this, and he felt like they're hassling people.

I explained to him that I understood, but he should check first. I said I didn't mind him asking questions but ask first before making a judgment. Unfortunately, I do feel like it's a little unsafe, and people now expect us to give that extra latitude—which kind of endangers us, and I almost feel like they want us to get shot and stabbed before they exonerate us. That's where the public is going, but that doesn't mean I don't have to do my job. But I love the fact that I was able to overcome that opposition, and now I feel like I had an impact on both of them. If I can just keep doing that every day, it will make a difference. If I don't know my community and have a connection with them, I may overact. If I can be proactive in reaching out, maybe we'll have less misjudging. We gotta win 'em back!

A Fresh Perspective –
More from Officer Ryan Tillman

By working as a black police officer, I started to see things from a different perspective. And that changed the way I saw law enforcement. That's why I created my own organization, Breaking Barriers United, with the sole purpose of bridging the gap between law enforcement and the community.[8] I started speaking in churches, and that led me to speaking in schools, and that led me to speaking in police departments. I started traveling around the country, and as that happened, I really started to change people's perspectives and the way they saw law enforcement. My goal is not to get you to become a fan of police; my goal is just to get you to have a different perspective. Throughout the COVID-19 pandemic, I have been able to do outreach virtually, which is phenomenal. That's how Brandon and I connected. We've been able to get our message out through social media.

I'm very excited that there are several voices out there—a lot through social media—who are offering different perspectives for black people. When you see people like Candace Owens, Brandon Tatum, Larry Elder, or Leo Terrell saying their opinion on what they think, it's encouraging as a black man because you know that you're not the only one. When you know there are others out there who stand by you, it empowers you.

I've also had some great experiences with policing that I'd like to share as hope for more positive encounters. One just happened recently, when we got a call for a guy who was in the middle of the street, and it looked like he was suicidal because he was trying to get hit by a car. I heard about it on the radio and called in to see if I could help. I'm trained on our crisis negotiation team. They invited me to come to see if I could help. When I arrived, the man, who happened to be black, was not listening to the police, and he refused to take his hands out of his pockets.

I ended up negotiating with this guy for about two and a half hours. He was definitely exhibiting some kind of mental issues. He wasn't responding to things I was asking him or telling him to do, but with the help of my partners getting information on who he was, I learned that he liked music, he produced R&B

---

8   Ryan Tillman, "Repairing the Bond between Law Enforcement and the Community," Breaking Barriers United, https://breakingbarriersunited.com/.

and hip hop, and that he loved jazz music. I kept talking to him and even played jazz music on my PA as a way to develop rapport. Of course, all these people are gathering and watching, like it's some kind of television show. After a while, nearly four hours in total, we had to use our less-lethal rounds on him so we could safely and successfully take him into custody. The most positive thing about it was all these people who were watching, including his family, contacted our police department and said what a phenomenal job we did with helping this guy. They were particularly impressed with my efforts to connect with him and do what I did for him. That was definitely a positive story.

Another time, I went to a mental health facility because we had to take a man into custody for threatening his family. He was also a black guy. They asked me to go there to assist. He had already assaulted some of the doctors, so we knew he was very violent. They had sedated him, and when I arrived, he was coming out of his sedation. I quickly developed a plan with my partners about what we were going to do and how we were going to take him into custody. But when we started to put our hands on him, he got very angry and tried to headbutt us, spit on us, and kick us. I just stayed calm and started talking to him. I reassured him that everything was okay, but he kept kicking at us. We had to put him on his stomach to put a hobble on him so he couldn't kick us. In order to do that, we had to put him on his stomach, and I had my knee across his back. Then he started saying, "I can't breathe. I can't breathe." So, I turned him on his side, and I explained, "Hey, man, this is what we're doing." Once I knew he was able to breathe, I put him back on his stomach, so we were able to get the hobble on him. As we were doing this, I was looking at him and started talking to him about his tattoos and making conversation and building a rapport with him by talking about his tattoos. About twenty minutes later, we were able to successfully get him into custody.

My sergeant has a customary practice to interview anyone that we use force on. So, he asked him directly, "Do you think our officers did anything wrong with you?"

He said, "Your officers were actually amazing. I love your officers—I actually have a problem with the doctors." But even the head of the doctors at the facility complimented the way we handled that situation and said it was flawless.

I wanted to share these stories because the general public usually only sees the ones that don't end well, like George Floyd and all the other polarizing ones. But these types of interactions happen more often than the negative ones; they just don't get the same coverage, which is sad because everybody bases their opinion on the negative ones that get all the press. That's why one of my biggest pushes now is getting some of these positive stories out there. I've already talked to my chief and my captain, and they agreed. So, over the course of the next year, we're going to start releasing more positive stories, and I believe you'll see other departments transition to this as well. I believe that is a step we can take for a fresh perspective and a more positive experience for black officers and all police offers.

Better Training and Self-Improvement – More from Officer Minner

I heard someone say that it takes more time to train to become a barber than it does to become a police officer. I looked it up, and yes, the initial training for both careers is six months, but for a cop, it doesn't stop there. After six months, you have three to four months more of field training where you're with someone else in the patrol car. You're trying to take what you learned and apply it. That's about ten months of training, and then there's an additional eight hours of training once a year. How much of that is critical training? Most cops are not going to get into a critical incident. The chances of a cop shooting someone is actually very rare. But that is the most critical part of what officers do. Say an officer has been on the force for ten years with no critical incidents. They've had their ten months of initial training, but then only eight hours a year for the next ten years. Everything else they have to learn on the fly. Then, on the tenth year, it's game time...critical incident...and he makes a mistake. So, who failed? Him? Or us for not giving him more critical incident training on a regular basis so that he's always mentally prepared for a crucial incident?

There needs to be training under stress, more firearms training. Training three or four times a year to start with, which I know is a big task. I wish we could provide training once a week, which is what I get to do in my current position. But it's not just more training; it's a shift in what's being trained and how frequently. It's super important, and I feel it's got to be done.

I already know I'm not the best guy out there, and I'm just scratching the surface of what I need to know to do my job to the best of my ability. I'm blessed to be on a team that trains every week; we shoot every week. But I have to take it upon myself to do more training. It's not enough to get your initial training and fire your gun once a year. I know there are too many cops who don't take it upon themselves to take a boxing class or a firearms class. They don't do it. And that's partly on the officer and partly on the agency. But these days, in our current society, nobody is gonna do it for you. Nobody's gonna back you up, and if you make a mistake, you're gonna get buried. You better have your ducks in a row and understand how to fight, how to take someone into custody, how to defend yourself, how to defend someone else, how to shoot...all that stuff. The days of *I meant well* are gone. If you make a mistake even in good faith, it's going to end up on the news, and public opinion is going to bury you.

Listen, there were tons of problems. I'm not saying don't fix those problems. I'm not saying don't reform law enforcement. There's a lot of issues that we've ignored. And if we have to change things, that's fine. But we can't change everything, certainly not all at once. And we don't need to be making a poor decision on what that change is because we've said yes to whatever someone else says who's being loud...to someone who just doesn't know what they're talking about because they don't have the experience. We must be logical and realistic about the progress and change.

Someone I respect told me that we are in customer service, and I get that. We need to do what we can to be sure people are satisfied with the service they're getting from law enforcement. That's not a bad thing. But you have to realize that it can be like a little kid asking for everything on every shelf in the store. Not everybody's gonna get what they ask for. Not everybody deserves to get what they're asking for, and not everybody's gonna be happy with the service. If you're being asked for something ridiculous, you can say no. We need to remember that we can say no. We're saying yes to everyone.

But I believe there is hope. I am a firm believer that there are always good people that will always do good despite adversity. Throughout history, in any group, in any profession, in any race, or any class, there have always been people within those groups that will stand up and go on to do a good job. Period. They didn't care what adversity they faced. They didn't stop and complain. They literally put their nose to the grindstone and got work done. I think the only hope that we have is that there are enough people out there like that, that will push on and turn things around. Included in those people is leadership, with enough good leaders stand up and say, *No* or *Enough*. I have a lot of good people here that are doing good work. And I don't mean just other cops, because alone we're not going to make the change. But the more everyday people can stand up and say no, that's not acceptable, the more people higher up will be able to say no as well.

I think it's a three-part solution. One is training from the bottom to the top—how we train and how often, so every officer is ready for those rare critical moments. Two is officer self-improvement—to take the steps to improve our abilities as officers individually. Three is individuals both in law enforcement and the public standing up—to not accept the blanket negative perception and to say no when no is called for.

Keep Reaching Out –
More from Officer Sean Payne

Even when I get discouraged, I never give up. There's been a lot of changes in policing over the last few years. Some of the changes, I think, are good, where some of the changes are only to pander to the Left's agenda. And while I have never abused my authority as far as overstepping or excessive use of force, I know some officers have overstepped those bounds. What I hope will make a difference is more transparency and education. Wait for all the facts to come out before rushing to judgment. Stop victimizing the criminals and stop giving them a platform to justify their wrongdoing. If the police are wrong, let the facts speak to that aspect and let the system do its job. Allowing the biased media to judge the actions of a police officer and portray them in a guilty light is wrong and scary. Moreover, and, likely, the biggest thing is more community involvement. What I mean is encouraging community members to join in on a ride-along or participate in police training. This idea builds relationships, support and gives the community a window into how police are trained and how we really do our job.

I said before that even when I arrest people, I hope I can make a positive difference in their lives. There was this one kid I arrested, and before I left him, I gave him my information. Then, I showed up in the courtroom at his sentencing hearing, and I said, "Dude, when you get out, if you want to change your path, reach out to me, and I will help you." He got out after three years and was on a six-month probation. The first person he called was his grandma. The second person he called was me. He says, "I want to change my path. I need your help. I need a job; it's going to be hard for me to get a job because I'm a felon." So fast-forward, I helped him get a job. He called me every day on FaceTime so I could see him, see that he was at home, not in trouble, and that he was doing good.

He *was* doing good, but he made a mistake. He was getting blowback from his crew for associating with the police, like he was a traitor. I'm not going to lie, the mistake he made was a serious felony. In the midst of him texting me and asking for help with his arrest, he made some threats toward me, and there was a hit put on me. Right then, my department wouldn't let me text or communicate with him anymore. So, he's reaching out to me because he needs help, but he's also got to protect himself and his reputation because he's definitely going back to prison. He's sending all these negative, threatening messages to me because he couldn't have others thinking he was friends with a cop. And I couldn't communicate with him because of that, and I had to protect my own family. I did try to send a message to him through his family, but I don't know if he ever got it. I share this story because I don't regret what I did. I would likely do it again. Yes, I have made some changes in what I do because I do not want my family to be in danger or ever feel threatened. But I will still reach out whenever and however I can to anyone I meet.

I also do outreach with the community, and I believe there's real power in that. On a simple level, a gentleman on Facebook was constantly attacking the police and questioning our decisions. One day I said, you know what, I'm going to get on Facebook and respond. I invited him on a ride-along. Long story short, he took me up on it, and his perspective changed. Now, we're friends.

Several years ago, our department started a program to invite community members to come out to the police academy and be role players for scenarios during officer training. They would play the roles of bad guys. We got an overwhelming response from the community; lots of people volunteered. At the end of each session, the community members, the trainee officers, and the academy staff would get together out in the courtyard, debrief the experience. That was such a positive way to connect and form bonds, and we provided an honest and positive experience. It changed minds; it created community. That program isn't active right now due to COVID, but my hope is that we can return to that someday soon.

My stories are just a few of the positive ways we can make a difference in the image of policing in America and the relationship between community and police. I refuse to give up hope, and I will always try to make a difference one person at a time.

Final Thoughts from Brandon Tatum

I echo what these officers have shared. For those who are already pro-police, please keep it up, and I thank you. For those who picked up this book and weren't so positive about police officers, I hope you've had some new thoughts. I hope that you've read this book with an open mind and an open heart. I truly hope your perspective is broader and more generous.

Now that you have been informed, entertained, and encouraged—be active. Be the change you want to see. It is up to us all to change the narrative. Race doesn't matter; class doesn't matter; your past doesn't matter. The only thing that matters is what you do after reading this book. Don't be afraid—be bold, be courageous.

For my officers out there: Hold the line. Never give up. Remember why you put on the badge. Remember that policing is not just a job but a calling in your life. God has positioned you for a time such as this to hold up the standard and to save your community from itself. Please, please, please, do me this last favor. Take care of yourself so that you can take care of others. Take time to reflect and relax and get away from it all when possible. Don't just have cop friends. Diversify your friends and your conversations. It's okay to cry. It's okay to be angry. It's okay to feel like you want to give up. But let that be a fart in the wind. And move on with confidence and faith. And know that B. Tatum has your six and will until they put me six feet under.

Once an officer, always a hero. Brandon Tatum

Afterword

Now anyone who has been following me for any length of time knows how I feel about the phrase *white privilege*. I think it is a myth and a made-up thing that does nothing more than further divide people in the country. It's rooted in hatred, deception, and division. I will tell you that I want to use swear words to describe how sick it makes me feel when people talk about white privilege. The last time I checked, we're all born the same way. In America, we all have the same rights and protections. The idea that all white people, regardless of their circumstances, are born with the same level of privilege that gives them an advantage over all black people is BS. Now, I know some people see me and say that I'm a sell-out because I don't categorize people based on their race. But it's just common sense because I'm not racist. I get offended when people say stupid things that are unjustified.

Instead of listening to other people and going along with what they say without thinking for myself, I base my thoughts on my personal experience. That may sound radical to some people who have forgotten how to think for themselves. Look, I knew many people back in the police department who were white. Some of them had stories about overcoming adversity that I will never be able to relate to because their socioeconomic situations just blew my mind. As a Black man in America, I have never had to deal with some of the things my white fellow police officers dealt with. So, when people bring up this false narrative that white people have privilege from birth, it's ridiculous.

Poverty does not care about the color of your skin. No matter who you are, what color your skin, you have to get up and make your way in the world. If you want to eat, put a roof over your head, and support your family, you have to go to work and earn a living. Yes, white privilege exists in isolated situations. There is also Black privilege in isolated situations. But there are people out there who want you to believe these different types of privilege exist so they can pit you against one another. Conservatives understand that we're all equal; we don't paint the picture that our country is dedicated to principles of privilege when they're not. Democrats do! They want you to believe it's racist to secure our southern border. They want to believe you're racist if you think everyone has the same opportunity but not guaranteed equity or results. In other words, everyone can get a job, but how successful you are will come down to how you apply yourself.

It's not just me. I recall an interview with Don Lemon and Morgan Freeman. Mr. Lemon kept trying to get Morgan Freeman to buy into how much harder it was for black people. Freeman noted that there they were, two quite successful black people. So it was clear there was opportunity for everyone. When Lemon asked a question about it being harder for black people to get out of those poorer communities, Morgan Freeman replied, "That bus runs twice a day." As I said, this is all about division and keeping people focused on our differences.

I was in a panel discussion recently, and a pastor on the panel was talking about all this white privilege. My response kind of shocked him until I followed it up with what I think is the kind of privilege we should be focusing on instead. It's Christ privilege.

If you're a Christian and you believe in Christ, it is time for you to be bold. None of us should be adhering to any other privilege except Christ privilege. If you are born in Christ, if you are in Christ Jesus, you are a new creation. If you are in Christ Jesus, then your privileges are now coming from God. They do not come from man anymore because how you get to God is through Christ. When you are in Christ, you have the privileges that God has afforded through Christ. Your privilege is Christ privilege, and I want people to understand that there ain't no job, no opportunity, no baby mama that matters more than the privileges, the grace, and the mercy coming from God.

And personally, I think God can still give you privileges even if you aren't in Christ, because God reigns on the just as well as the unjust. That's what the Bible says. You have an expected hope that you will have a privilege in Christ Jesus. There is power and hope and opportunity and blessings in the inheritance of Christ privilege. I want people to understand this. I know I'm kind of preaching here and speaking to the people who have been saved, but you already know my testimony. I think too many of us have disconnected from the spiritual realm. We focus on the news and social media and Hollywood to give us our focus, and we forfeit our souls in the process. I think people forget sometimes that there is God in heaven who made the heavens and earth.

I get it. The human condition, the world we live in, seems to get crazier and harder every day. It seems that there is no hope left, but we keep searching for it. Our search gets disrupted by our culture. Our culture feeds on our hatred. There are too many false messages out there pointing out our differences. Someone is benefiting from people taking sides and hating others. Someone is making bank by creating victims and then selling some kind of solution to those fake victims. And when people like me come along and point out the deception, they are shut down, canceled, and silenced. I pray that more people are starting to wake up and smell the deception. The division between us is false and will begin to fade away as we think for ourselves. For me, I believe that when we focus on what brings us together—our Christ privilege—we will make this world a better place for everyone. I believe it so much that I made a Christ privilege t-shirt. I say this not to try to sell you anything but to let you know I stand with this belief enough to put it in writing!